LIFE

TO

THE

FULLEST

LIFE

TO

THE

FULLEST

YOUR BEST IS YET TO COME!

BRYANT WESTBROOK

PALMETTO
PUBLISHING
Charleston, SC
www.PalmettoPublishing.com

Hardcover ISBN: 979-8-8229-3290-6
Paperback ISBN: 979-8-8229-3291-3
eBook ISBN: 979-8-8229-3292-0

There are a couple of people to thank for bringing this book to life. Thanks to Kimberly Davies for your diligent work editing this book. You brought great insight and sophistication to this project. Thank you to Palmetto Publishing for helping me get this book published. Your support and guidance have been special to me. Lastly, to Allison. You've been with me through many changes in life and have given me great support. I am grateful for your love, encouragement and how you make me a better husband and follower of Jesus.

TABLE OF CONTENTS

Author's Note   i

Part 1: You Are Loved   1
    You Are Custom-Made   3
    The Love Of The Father   12
    The Work of the Savior   25
    Accepting the Savior   36

Part 2: Life With the Savior   51
    Knowing Your Identity   53
    Talking to Jesus Part 1   63
    Talking to Jesus Part 2   73
    Faith for _____.   87

Part 3: Living For the Savior   103
    Sinful Nature Vs. Spiritual Nature   105
    Daily Battles   113
    Don't Fight Alone   127
    Living on a Mission   137

Encouragement   145
Next Steps   147
About the Author   149
Connect   150

AUTHOR'S NOTE

Several years ago, I began to have a strong desire within my heart—a desire for God to use my story to inspire and empower others to live life to the fullest. Through prayer and dedication, this book evolved from a mere idea into a tangible reality.

This journey has demanded an immense amount of effort, numerous revisions, and, truthfully, some tears shed while translating the stories onto paper. My hope and prayer is that this book will assist you in experiencing the fullness of life with Jesus as your Savior.

Every chapter has been written with this aspiration in mind. Throughout this process, I've continually revisited this core reason behind this book's creation.

This purpose has not only kept me grounded but also fueled my excitement about its message. I hope that as you read, my heartfelt intention becomes more evident to you, providing you with insight on my experience.

In addition to my overarching purpose, I have also been praying that two scriptures would illuminate your heart as you read:

Unless the Lord builds the house, the builders labor in vain. (Psalm 127:1a, NIV)

Therefore, if anyone is in Christ, the new creation has come: The old has gone, the new is here! (2 Corinthians 5:17, NIV)

Part of my prayerful desire is that this book will assist you in constructing a life where Jesus is the foundation. Life at its fullest commences with Jesus, and without Jesus it's impossible to attain. He is the ultimate architect, the master builder, eager to underpin and contribute to every facet of our lives.

Thank you for embarking on this journey with me. As you dive into its pages and discover what the Lord has in store for you, I genuinely believe, with all my heart, that your brightest days lie ahead, not behind. Jesus has a life to the fullest awaiting you!

The best is yet to come!

Bryant

PART 1:

YOU

ARE

LOVED

YOU ARE CUSTOM-MADE

Since my earliest memories, there's been one phrase that has echoed through my life, never wavering, never fading into the background. It's a phrase that's followed me relentlessly, and no matter how many years have gone by, the phrase never goes away.

This phrase echoes, "You look just like your mom!" And believe me when I say, it's not an exaggeration; I truly resemble my mom, almost like a guy version of her! It's something that everyone who has ever crossed paths with both of us has pointed out. My mom beams with pride at this resemblance, and I couldn't be prouder to be her son.

During my upbringing, whether it was a routine doctor's visit or a dental checkup, every time my mom and I went together, I always heard the same chorus, "You two look just alike!" And every new school year, from elementary to high school, during those nerve-racking open house events, I'd hear it once again, "You really do resemble your mama, young man!"

I have to admit, during my middle school years, it used to irritate me a bit. At that age, you're on the journey of self-discovery, and the last thing you want is to be perceived as an extension of someone else. It's a phase of life when you're striving to carve out your own identity, yearning to be known for just being you.

Now, years have passed, and I find myself living in Kansas, a world away from my Georgia roots. My mom still lives in Georgia, and I make it a point to visit whenever I can, usually during the blissful summer breaks or the heartwarming holiday season.

I'll never forget a couple of years ago when my wife, Allison and I were getting ready to fly back home from Georgia. It was my mom who drove us to the airport in Greenville, South Carolina. When we parked the car and strolled up to the Delta counter, the Delta agent looked at me first and then my mom. She chimed in with a friendly remark: "That's really sweet of you to bring your little brother to the airport." I couldn't help but think, "Seriously?" Oh, I almost forgot one important detail—it's not just that we resemble each other, but we also look quite youthful!

We appear so young that the agent assumed we were siblings. I couldn't even fathom who she thought Allison was! My mom calmly asserted, "I'm his mom." The agent, somewhat amazed, commented, "Wow! You two just look so alike each other, I thought you were brother and sister."

The uncanny resemblance to my mom is something that I'll carry with me throughout my life, regardless of how many birthdays come and go. I'll never outgrow it, and I'll never be able to escape it. Her likeness is a permanent part of me.

Perhaps you too bear a striking resemblance to your mom, dad, a grandparent, or even a sibling. If so, I can certainly empathize, and I'm sending some positive thoughts your way! I've heard it said that each of us has a twin somewhere in the world, and that's probably true. However, if that's the case, I haven't stumbled upon mine yet, aside from my mom, of course.

Just as I resemble my mom, you also share a remarkable likeness with someone out there. In fact, the resemblance might be even more remarkable than you can imagine.

You weren't mass-produced on an assembly line; you were carefully and perfectly designed to bear a resemblance to the Creator. Recognizing and embracing this truth is where the journey to living life to its fullest truly begins.

MADE IN THE IMAGE OF GOD

Now, if you've never heard before that you were created in the image and likeness of God, it might sound a bit astonishing. You could be wondering, "Are you telling me that I resemble God? How can that be?" Let's embark on a little journey together with an open heart and mind.

You bear a resemblance to the Creator of the moon, stars, planets, and all that surrounds us. What's truly remarkable about the Creator is the meticulous care with which He fashions His designs. When God fashioned the world, this is how the book of Genesis describes it:

> In the beginning God created the heavens and the earth. Now the earth was formless and empty, darkness was over the surface of the deep, and the Spirit of God was hovering over the waters. And God said, "let there be light," and there was light. God saw that the light was good, and he separated the light from the darkness. (Genesis 1:2-4 NIV)

Here, we witness the Creator crafting light and darkness from nothing. Contemplating the sun and how it bathes our planet in light is nothing short of breathtaking. The sun's precise position in space, just the right distance from earth, is a miracle in itself. I once read that if it were any closer, our planet would scorch under its heat. No human can even conceive the design that takes to pull off. From mountains and valleys to deserts, everything is uniquely fashioned.

Few experiences can match the beauty of a sunset: the sky painted in shades of orange and purple, adorned with big, fluffy white clouds. Whether it's a brisk fall morning or a scorching summer day, we are blessed to relish this magnificent creation together. As God created light and darkness and declared them good, He continued to shape the earth, filling it with vegetation and populating the oceans with diverse marine life. In the book of Psalms, we are reminded:

> The earth is the Lord's, and everything in it. The world and all its people belong to him. For he laid the earth's foundation on the seas and built it on the ocean depths. (Psalm 24:1-2 NLT)

God's creative work didn't stop with the universe; His creation continued because He knew that His most treasured creation was yet to—come, and this most treasured creation was humanity. Notice the second sentence in the verse above: "all its people belong to him."

Have you ever eaten a delicious meal? And while savoring this delicious meal you were eagerly anticipating the best part, which is the dessert? That's me every time I know there's dessert involved; I can't help myself because I know the best is for last. Especially if it's something made out of chocolate—that's speaking my love language!

Here's how the Bible describes the creation of humanity, after everything else was created. After God had finished creating the world, the animals, and space as if He hadn't shown off enough already, He really shows off here. He saves the best for last!

God spoke, saying, "Let us make human beings in our image, make them reflect our nature. So they can be responsible for the fish in the sea, the birds in the air, the cattle,

And, yes, Earth itself, and every animal that moves on the face of Earth." God created human beings; he created them godlike, Reflecting God's nature. He created them male and female. (Genesis 1:26-28a MSG)

Humanity is more like God than anything else He's ever created. We resemble God more than the earth, the sun, the planets, the ocean, or any living creature you can think of. God chose you to mirror His image because He loves you more than anything else. The scripture above conveys that God created us in His nature and what that means is God put things in us so that we would resemble Him.

God gave us what's called communicable attributes, or to put it simply, ways we are similar to God. It's like when you create something, whether it's a piece of pottery, a drawing on paper, or a canvas painting—you place your signature on it so people can recognize you as the author. That's exactly what God did with us.

You resemble God more than you can even imagine! We've seen the word "image" appear in the verses above; in Hebrew, the word for "image" is "tselem," which means "similar." You are uniquely crafted in the image of God, and you reflect who God is!

The tricky part is, many of us in today's world don't realize this. We often believe we're just the result of our parents or upbringing and nothing more. But that couldn't be further from the truth.

Let me show you some of the ways we share similarities with God:

1. Righteousness

Since the day you were born, you instinctively knew how to misbehave! No one needed to teach you how to toss your peas and carrots onto the floor, or how to nibble on people's fingers.

As you grew up, you became aware of your wrongdoings and began to discern right from wrong. Chances are, you observe injustices in the world around you. It might trouble you to realize that injustice exists, but you can distinguish it because of God. God is a just God. He loves justice and righteousness. We possess an innate sense of what's right, even though we don't always act accordingly. This sense of righteousness comes from God, who is inherently just and right. This longing in us for justice is directly fashioned in us from God.

Righteousness and justice are the foundation of your throne. Unfailing love and truth walk before you as attendants. (Psalm 89:14 NLT)

2. Love

Love is at the core of God's essence, and He was the first to love. We, too, have the capacity to love because God loves first. He was the first to love. We share this attribute with God because we have the ability to feel and show love. There are people in your life whom you hold dear—siblings, aunts, uncles, cousins, spouses, or perhaps even your beloved pet. I understand the last one completely; I adore my dog, Riley. Our ability to love is a gift from God, instilled within us.

We love because he first loved us. (1 John 4:19 NIV)

3. Knowledge

A word often used to describe God is "omniscience," which means all-knowing. God embodies knowledge, possessing awareness of everything there is to know. He has bestowed this quality upon us, enabling us to acquire knowledge as well. We engage in hobbies to improve our skills, and we apply knowledge in our daily careers to make informed decisions. Our capacity to gain knowledge and wisdom is a gift from God.

For the Lord gives wisdom; from his mouth come knowledge and understanding (Proverbs 2:6 NIV)

The most fundamental parts and abilities you possess are a direct reflection of the One who loves you unconditionally. Your creation was purposeful, with careful thought and intention. If such profound consideration was given to your creation, imagine the intention behind the life you lead.

Consider these words from God after He crafted humanity:

God saw all that he had made, and it was very good. And there was evening, and there was morning—the sixth day. (Genesis 1:31, NIV)

Let me draw your attention to something here: as we read through the creation story together, did you notice what God said each time He created something? He repeated the same word over and over again when something new came into existence:

God created the light and darkness, and He said it was "good."

God created the ocean and all the animals in it and said it was "good."

God made the sun and all the birds in the air and said it was "good."

It's interesting to pause here and acknowledge that God was pleased with His creation. He was pleased because we understand that you don't call something good unless you truly believe and experience how good it is. However, there's something different when He created humanity. Did you notice it earlier? God never described anything as "very good" until He made Man. He said it then, and He's saying it now when He looks at you, saying, "Wow, look at him. Very good." "Wow, take a look at her. Very good."

Friend, don't underestimate yourself as average or ordinary. You are not. You are above average, the pinnacle of God's creation. God is not just the Creator of everything; He is also a loving father. He can be the most loving father you could ever have if you open your heart to Him. Remember this:

You don't just reflect God; you were made
to know God and be loved by God.

In the next chapter, we'll dive into how God is a loving father who desires a relationship with you. He longs for you to know Him and to be an active part of your life. God didn't end with giving you qualities that resemble Him; He deeply cares about you. His heart aches for you, and He eagerly desires to be with you in your everyday life.

I recently visited a massive aquarium in Oklahoma, and there, I noticed a parent who had lost their child. The father was frantically searching everywhere, calling out his son's name, looking under tables, and asking people if they had seen his son. The terror on the father's face was evident.

All he wanted was to be reunited with his son. When this man's son was born, he didn't say, "OK, that's good; I can stop loving this child now." Instead, he vowed to love and protect His child. All this dad in the aquarium wanted was to be with his son. The same holds true for you as God is your loving father; all He desires is to be with you. He's actively searching for you, patiently waiting, and He deeply loves you.

I recently returned home to Georgia for one of those summer visits. At age twenty-nine, I'm not a kid anymore, and I'm a little older than when those stories took place above. When I returned home, I went with my brother, Kenly, to a local restaurant called Cafe Silo. There, we settled in to eat some good food; we each also ordered a glass of ice-cold southern sweet tea. As we enjoyed our meal, a man walked in.

I had never met this man before, I couldn't tell who he was or what his name was but guess what he said to me? He said, "I know who you are just by the look of your face, boy. You're Lisa's son ain't ya?"

I replied, "Yes, sir, that's right. How did you know?"

He simply said, "You look just like her."

Just like I will never outgrow looking like my mom, we'll never outgrow reflecting God. Chances are you've lived your whole life and have never thought about how you resemble God. Just like you'll never outgrow resembling God, you'll never outgrow His love for you. I can't wait to keep going on this journey with you!

Now, let's take a few moments to reflect on what you've just read. Consider these questions and jot down your thoughts to keep track:

MOMENT OF REFLECTION

- Have you ever contemplated God as Creator?

- How does it make you feel knowing that God crafted you with intention?

- How does it make you feel that when God created the first humans, He declared them "very good"? Do you believe this statement about yourself? Why or why not?

- How might understanding the content of this first chapter reshape your view of God and yourself?

THE LOVE
OF THE FATHER

There are many people in my life that I love, and I'd like to introduce you to a couple of them:

First, there's my beloved grandma, Diane. She played a significant role in my upbringing, always there to care for me. I have fond memories of Grandma Diane teaching me how to drive, allowing me to take the wheel of her Jeep Cherokee in her yard. After my laps around her yard, she would treat me to shopping trips in Commerce, Georgia, where we explored our favorite stores.

Also, my dad Shannon for spending time with me when I was younger by coaching me in baseball, taking me to see the Atlanta Braves, the Yankees and the Gwinnett Braves play. We would also go and try different restaurants together and go shopping often. I'm grateful for the quality time my dad spent with me while growing up.

Next, I'm grateful for my Papa Bill. He and I spent a lot of quality time together. Papa Bill introduced me to the world of NASCAR, a passion I still indulge in, particularly when races happen at Daytona Motor Speedway. He also sparked my interest in military history, and I'm a sucker for a good history lesson or a visit to a history museum.

My stepdad, Ken, for his unwavering support and his willingness to travel to Kansas multiple times to visit and help with household tasks. You see, I'm not particularly handy, I once was sent to the hardware store to get nails and I may have gone back with screws. I'm grateful for his support in this way as you can tell!

Then, there's Allison, who came into my life like a burst of sunshine. I had never known I could feel such profound love for another person. She is, without a doubt, the greatest gift and blessing I've ever received. It's amusing because I declared my love for her just a month after meeting her. It's a wonder she stuck around! I'm eternally grateful for the ways she enriches my life. Her talents, love, support, and encouragement are truly priceless.

Perhaps you've experienced a similar kind of love, maybe from your parents or grandparents during your upbringing. It's the kind of love that makes you feel cherished and safe.

This kind of love can also extend to someone like a son, daughter, niece, nephew, or even a mentor. It's the love of someone who takes you under their wing, protects you, and guides you.

There are many ways we can feel loved and give love, just like I have explained about my life. You recognize love when it's present—the warm feeling in your heart, the fluttering butterflies in your stomach, the euphoria in your mind. Love is truly amazing. Love is a force to be reckoned with.

Contemplating the power of love leads me to reflect on how much God must love the world and us to create such incredible things.

WHAT'S YOUR IMAGE OF GOD?

Up to this point we've considered how God views us. Now, I invite you to think about your perception of God. We know now what God thinks of us, but what do you think of Him? How do you picture God and what thoughts come to mind? Are they positive or negative? What emotions and feelings wash over you when you contemplate God?

While growing up, my perception of God took on various forms. I used to believe that God's mood fluctuated, sometimes displeased with me, and happy with me during other times. But my most common thought back then was that God was merely a Sunday-morning obligation, forgotten about for the rest of the week.

I recall attending a particular church with my family in my upbringing. It was a small congregation, and every Sunday, a group of kind-hearted ladies from the church would treat us to homemade muffins and biscuits. Those delectable breakfast treats became the highlight of my Sundays, often motivating me to get out of bed even when I didn't feel like it. I would often think, certainly, God is more than just good people and delicious pastries, right? However, this notion that God was limited to just one hour on Sundays felt incomplete.

YOU LIKELY HAVE YOUR OWN PERCEPTION OF GOD, AS WELL

When you hear the words "God" and "Heavenly Father," certain thoughts or experiences come to mind. Perhaps, like me, you didn't ponder much about God or His thoughts while growing up. Maybe you, too, believed or still believe that He's reserved solely for Sunday gatherings. Someone who encourages you to have a hearty breakfast and good company for that hour before you head home. It's possible that attending church was driven by feelings of guilt, the fear that God would somehow "punish" you if you didn't show up. Maybe when you think of God you associate the word "work" with Him meaning God wants you to work harder and do better. Maybe you went to church weekly because there was a girl or guy you found attractive there—not the worst place to meet someone, I suppose.

Or perhaps, growing up, you had a drug problem, meaning your parents "drug" you to church every Sunday and you didn't like it! Undoubtedly, the experiences you've had in church have molded your perception of God, and that's perfectly understandable. Some of you might even envision God as an angry and furious entity. I can relate to that perspective. Allow me to share a personal story from my younger days. I remember when I was about twelve years old, someone invited my family to join them at their church. We attended the service, and everything seemed to be running smoothly.

People appeared friendly, but I still had my guard up. At that age, I had limited experience with church attendance, and I was cautious. When the music began to play, a crowd of people surged forward, and the preacher took the stage, erupting into a rage-like passionate sermon. His face turned beet red, sweat poured down like rain, and his voice thundered across the room. He began screaming at the top of his lungs. It was a sight to behold. He laid his hands on the congregation, and they responded with equal tension. Because of all the screaming I was led to believe that God was mad at everyone there. I sat in my pew, overwhelmed by the intensity of the moment, unsure of what I was witnessing. That day, as I left the church, I was left with more questions than answers. I couldn't help but wonder, "Is God really that angry? That must mean that He's angry with me too?" For a season, this made me think God was all about anger.

Perhaps, like many today, you envision God as a distant figure, disconnected from the world's realities. You might see Him as a heavenly record-keeper, meticulously noting every misstep and waiting to exact punishment, like Santa Claus with a year-long naughty list. The thought of every wrong you've ever committed being documented can be daunting. It's possible that you perceive God as profoundly disappointed in you, believing your wrongs outweigh your rights, making it impossible for you to be in good standing within His presence.

Alternatively, you may doubt God's existence, considering the possibility of multiple gods from various religions. You might even think that when life ends, it's all over, period. For you, when you contemplate God's thoughts about you, you might wrestle with feelings of shame. It might be due to something you did, or something done to you, but that sense of shame is undeniably real and valid.

Perhaps you're carrying the weight of shame from last night, two weeks ago, or even a distant memory from thirty-one years ago. Your emotions are genuine, and I want to acknowledge that. What you're feeling is real.

Or it could be that you grew up without a father who expressed pride in you, leading you to believe that God couldn't possibly be proud of you either. These are deep and heartfelt concerns.

Once, I had someone tell me, back when I was younger, that following God boils down to doing all the right things and being completely obedient to Him. But what if you find yourself not doing the right thing? Does that mean God's angry with you? Does it mean He doesn't care, and you're left feeling unloved and undervalued?

Then, there are some of you who might associate God with a lack of love due to a painful loss. It could have been your spouse (and even thinking about this is painful—I can't imagine how that must feel; if this is your story, I'm truly sorry). It could have been a parent or guardian. It might have been a grandparent with whom you shared a deep bond while growing up, or perhaps a close friend. Whoever it was, you may feel that God took them away or didn't heal them, leaving you with a deep resentment toward Him.

Lastly, it might be the everyday struggles you face on this earthly journey that make you question whether God cares at all. Rent is always looming and money is in short supply. The cost of food keeps rising, the car payment is overdue, and it feels like you're drowning. All of this can lead to the thought, "If God is real and loving, why isn't He providing for me?"

It's possible to see Him as a Creator but not provider, powerful but not forgiving, loving but seemingly not present enough to intervene powerfully in your life. We all paint different pictures of God in our minds, influenced by our unique perspectives and personal circumstances. That's the point I want to stress: we each have our own opinions about God, shaped by our life experiences.

Here's a simple exercise I'd like you to try with me right now. Take your current thoughts and opinions about God and set them aside. Open your hand, and silently tell yourself, "I'm going to be open-minded about God from this day forward." Even this small act can bring you a bit of peace, loosening your grip and allowing your heart to open.

You see, God is far grander than any mental box we try to place Him in. He's beyond the limits of our descriptive words. A friend of mine, Andy, once shared some wisdom with me: "You'll never draw closer to God by confining Him within the boundaries of your mind, because He's infinitely greater than that."

Do you recall when we contemplated the act of creation and marveled at how God created everything else before us? He sculpted the stars, molded the seas, breathed life into animals, and adorned the world with landscapes ranging from towering mountaintops to serene valleys.

I used to live in Alaska, and I was constantly captivated by its beauty. During my time in Alaska, I found myself irresistibly drawn to the outdoors. I would embark on adventures in my trusty Jeep, seeking out remote spots where I could simply bask in nature's grandeur. There, I would sit in quiet reverence, gazing in wonder at the magnificent snowy peaks as they embrace the sun.

I had never before encountered such a profoundly creative environment. The sight of moose and the various kinds of wildlife that call Alaska home left me speechless. In those moments, Alaska opened my mind up to comprehend the vastness of God's creation. I just couldn't help but to be out in nature just be in complete wonder of God.

We often stand in awe of nature, declaring it as the pinnacle of existence, yet we sometimes lose sight of the divine order of creation. We forget what came first and what came last. It wasn't those majestic mountains, nor the graceful birds soaring in the sky. No, that came first. The final masterpiece, the crowning achievement, was us. God, in His wisdom, saved humanity for last. Let us remember that God created us, and His declaration was unequivocal: "very Good."

WHO GOD IS

I'll never forget my brother's friend, Stoney. He was persistent, relentlessly inviting my brother to attend NewSpring Church in Anderson, South Carolina, every week when my brother and I were in high school. I recall my brother returning home after several weeks of attending and urging me to join him. I hesitated initially, mainly because of my previous church experiences.

Despite my reluctance, I ultimately accepted their invitation due to their persistence. It was in May of 2013 when I first stepped into

NewSpring. Little did I know that this experience would transform my life, and I had no inkling of what God had in store for me.

For approximately four months, I attended and during that time, I started sensing something profound happening within my heart. It was a peculiar feeling, something I had never experienced in my eighteen years of life.

Gradually, I came to realize that it was God at work in my heart. There was no other way to describe it. He was gently tugging at my heartstrings, vying for my attention. Week after week, this tug grew stronger and stronger, and I vividly recall someone saying in one of the messages, "God is trying to get your attention because He loves you."

After five months of experiencing this inner stirring and engaging in heartfelt conversations with small group leaders at the church, I came to understand that God had been pursuing my heart all along. The way Jesus was shared with me was unlike I had ever heard before. Jesus was shared as a God of love and care for me. Jesus was shared as someone who wanted something for me not from me. Jesus was shared as someone wanting me to truly have life to the fullest.

It was during this time that I encountered a potent form of God's love, a love I had never comprehended before. It boiled down to this: God pursued me relentlessly. At first, I didn't seek God; it was the other way around. He kept chasing after me until He finally had my full attention.

I was experiencing a love so profound that I began to grasp the true meaning of these verses:

Because God is love. This is how God showed his love among us: He sent his one and only Son into the world that we might live through him. (1 John 4:8b-9 NIV)

And may you have the power to understand, as all God's people should, how wide, how long, how high, and how deep his love is. (Ephesians 3:18 NLT)

God is love. He is the source of love. He has loved us way before you or I ever knew what love was. His love is deep for you because He cares about every part of your life. God is love, and His love for you knows no bounds. If you are holding this book and reading it, it's no coincidence. It suggests that, just like me, God has been pursuing you too. You're not randomly stumbling upon this message about His love. Perhaps like me, you need to read this sentence one more time:

God is trying to get your attention because He loves you.

Perhaps you've walked with Jesus for a long time but have forgotten how cherished you are. Allow God to remind you that His love for you has never waned. You might be someone who feels empty inside, seeking answers to fill that void. Perhaps someone thought you needed to read this, and they gave it to you as a gift. Or maybe, you discovered it in an unexpected place (hopefully not in the trash). It could be that you've known God for years, but your perception of Him is skewed, and God wants to transform that image.

Alternatively, you may have never given much thought to God or His love for you, but today, you are pondering it. However, this book found its way into your hands, and I wholeheartedly believe that you hold it for a purpose. God is relentlessly pursuing you, and the reason is simple—He loves you deeply.

One of the remarkable aspects of Jesus's teachings is how He portrayed God when people inquired about Him. On numerous occasions, Jesus lovingly referred to God as our "Father." In response to a question about how to address God, He shared these profound words:

This, then, is how you should pray: 'Our Father in heaven, hallowed be your name.' (Matthew 6:9a NIV)

This depiction of God as a Father underscores an essential truth: before anything else, God is your loving Father. He is eager to connect with you and desires to spend time in your presence.

God not only sees you, but He also knows you intimately. He genuinely cares about every aspect of your life, even the smallest details. He understands your aspirations, dreams, and the goals you seek to achieve.

Before Jesus embarked on His ministry of healing and performing miracles, He was baptized. The significance lies in the words spoken by God the Father during that momentous occasion, as recorded in the book of Matthew:

> As soon as Jesus was baptized, he went up out of the water. At that moment heaven was opened, and he saw the Spirit of God descending like a dove and alighting on him. And a voice from heaven said, "This is my Son, whom I love; with him I am well pleased." (Matthew 3:16-17 NIV)

These words underscore the unwavering love God has for His son, Jesus Christ—a love not based on any deeds or accomplishments. In the same way, God loves you unconditionally. You don't need to earn His love or strive for perfection. God isn't waiting for you to have your life perfectly organized or somehow work your way into a prosperous and better life before He can bless you.

God is not waiting for your child to make better choices or until you complete your degree or achieve your goals and ambitions before He can use you for His Divine works. God is not waiting for you to reconcile that relationship before He bestows His endless love upon you. God is saying to you right now:

My child, I knew you before you were born. I am a loving Father who loves you as my child, and I don't hate you. I am always knocking at the door of your heart, my arms are always open to receive you. I love and care for you, and I want you to listen to my voice. My child, do not be afraid for I am with you. Call upon me and I will answer you. I want a relationship with you. I want to be in relationship with you for I will bless you abundantly with endless love and abundant grace.

In essence, God's love for you is constant and unwavering, just as it was for Jesus. He longs to be a part of your journey, regardless of where you stand today. So, embrace His love, knowing that you are cherished beyond measure. God's love for you is unwavering, and His care for you is boundless. He wants you to know this with all certainty. God is not angry with you; rather, He yearns to love and care for you. He desires a deep, meaningful relationship with you and He has overflowing love and grace for you." God's love for you knows no bounds; He is not disappointed in you but deeply enamored by you. Even before you graced this earthly realm with your presence, God's love for you was already in motion, and there is absolutely nothing you could ever say or do to diminish His love for you.

I once heard a preacher during a sermon say, "God knew every foolish and sinful thing you would ever do, say, or even think, and yet here you stand. He still chose to create you, to breathe life into you, and to shower you with His boundless love."

God is a Father to the fatherless, a defender of widows, residing in His holy sanctuary (See Psalm 68:5). He yearns to guide you, protect you, and shower you with His love.

Instead, God takes immense pleasure in you and eagerly desires to draw you near to Him. He stands by your side, supporting and championing you. I am reminded of the words of Jesus when He spoke to a group of people grappling with life's perplexing questions, much like you and me. They fretted over tangible concerns such as paying next month's rent, fixing broken things, confronting seemingly insurmountable tasks at work, and gathering clothes for their children. These are the real, everyday challenges we all face.

Jesus says in Matthew 6:25-27 (NIV), "Therefore I tell you, do not worry about your life, what you will eat or drink; or about your body, what you will wear. Is not life more than food, and the body more than clothes? Look at the birds of the air; they do not sow or reap or store away in barns, and yet your heavenly Father feeds them. Are you not much more valuable than they? Can any one of you by worrying add a single hour to your life?"

True freedom, wholeness, and security come from finding rest in your Heavenly Father's embrace and allowing Him to care for you. He is the Father you've always needed, and you don't need to convince Him otherwise. He is the ultimate provider, the one who restores beauty from the broken pieces of your past. His forgiveness soothes your weary heart, and His strength empowers you to keep moving forward. God's love for you knows no bounds; He's willing to move mountains to be with you, breaking through any barriers that stand in His way. God holds you in high regard and eagerly anticipates your future.

> As a father has compassion on his children, so the Lord has compassion on those who fear him. (Psalm 103:13 NIV)

God is eager to pour out His love and compassion on you. He isn't waiting to repay you for your mistakes; that's not who He is. God is a God of mercy, peace, grace, and boundless love.

This chapter brings to mind a recent experience Allison and I had while house hunting. We learned more than we ever thought we would about markets, interest rates, and houses. One thing we noticed was that some houses had significant issues. For instance, we came across a house with a terrible foundation—a massive, unmistakable hole in the back. It was an eyesore, and our realtor wisely steered us away from it. We encountered houses that emitted foul odors and needed extensive, costly repairs.

Allison and I decided to pass on these houses because we realized we weren't meant to delve into such messes, especially when we lacked the financial means to address those problems. Perhaps you feel the same way about yourself. You might believe that you have a metaphorical "gaping hole" within you, that the damage is too extensive and expensive to fix.

You might even think that God views you in the same way we viewed those houses—unworthy of His love, too far gone to be redeemed. But that couldn't be further from the truth.

God not only welcomes your mess but actively invites it into His presence. Even a shattered and crumbling foundation doesn't deter God in the slightest. Whether you're drowning in thousands or even millions of dollars of debt, it doesn't intimidate God—He is the ultimate provider.

There is absolutely nothing in your life that can scare God away. His deepest desire is to draw close to you. I'm profoundly thankful that God's love for us isn't based on our performance or perfection; it's rooted in the fact that He's a loving Father who desires the best for His children.

I remember when I felt God tugging at my heart. It was crystal clear to me that God wanted a relationship with me. He had my full attention, and I knew I needed to respond. Consider this book as God's way of trying to capture your attention. I had some burning questions about God and His love for me. I wondered, "How could I invite God into my life? What steps could I take to allow God's love to flood into my heart?" I had to confront something known as sin—the barrier between me and the Father, preventing me from having a close relationship with Him. It's not just me; it's you too. Sin is what's holding us back from experiencing the incredible love God has for us. But fret not, there's a way to overcome sin, and we'll explore it in the next chapter.

MOMENT OF REFLECTION

Remember that God is on your side, not against you. His love for you is unwavering, and He desires a meaningful relationship with you. As you delve into this chapter, reflect on a few questions to help you connect with these profound concepts.

- Firstly, consider the thoughts you held about God before entering this chapter. Have they evolved or deepened in any way? Has your understanding of God become more profound?

- Take a moment to think about any scripture or story that resonated with you while reading. Did any particular passage touch your heart or provide a new perspective on God's love and grace?

- Furthermore, ponder whether this chapter has altered your perception of God. Have you gained a fresh outlook on His character, His intentions, or His role in your life?

- Consider how you feel about God's care for you. Do you sense a deeper level of His affection and concern? Are you experiencing a more profound connection with Him as a result of your insights from this chapter?

- Lastly, reflect on your motivation. Are you living your life seeking approval from God, or are you living it knowing you already have His approval? Recognizing the difference can bring about a profound shift in your relationship with Him.

- In exploring these questions, you'll not only gain a deeper understanding of your own spirituality but also nurture a closer connection with the loving presence of God in your life.

THE WORK
OF THE SAVIOR

The Burj Khalifa, situated in the heart of Dubai, United Arab Emirates, proudly holds the title of the world's tallest building. This majestic structure soars to heights that often carry it above the clouds, truly embracing its role as a skyscraper extraordinaire. It's important to note that the Burj Khalifa is not just any ordinary building; its developers had a grand vision, and they succeeded in creating the tallest building on the planet. Rising to an astounding height of 2,722 feet with a remarkable one hundred, sixty-three floors, the Burj Khalifa's construction journey began in January 2004, starting with the foundation and groundwork. It finally reached completion in January 2010, a monumental six-year undertaking. The sheer scale of this building is nothing short of awe-inspiring.

Within its colossal frame, the Burj Khalifa houses residences, offices, and observation points that beckon tourists from around the globe. Indeed, it is a must-visit destination for anyone traveling to or through the Middle East. I, too, aspire to witness its grandeur someday. To put its enormity into perspective, consider that the One World Trade Center in New York City stands at 1,776 feet and boasts one hundred and four floors, an impressive structure in its own right but dwarfed by the Burj Khalifa.

My personal experience with towering structures led me to the Willis Tower in Chicago, Illinois. Completed in 1974, it reaches a substantial height of 1,450 feet and comprises one hundred and ten floors. At the time of its completion, it held the distinction of being the world's tallest building.

One of the most thrilling features of the Willis Tower is the Skydeck, located on its one hundred and third floor. The Skydeck offers an exhilarating experience as it extends beyond the building's edge, encased in thick glass casing. Stepping onto this transparent platform provides an unparalleled sensation of standing in midair. During my first visit to the Skydeck, I was filled with a mixture of excitement and fear. As I tiptoed onto the glass, I could feel it shifting beneath my feet. Gazing downward, I saw a staggering one hundred and three floors of open air with people and cars on the street far below. My heart sank as I thought about how there was nothing but a pain of glass standing between me and the concrete below. To my surprise, a young child joined me in the glass, and what ensued was nothing short of heart-pounding.

The child began jumping up and down vigorously, causing the glass beneath us to tremble. Panic welled up within me, my stomach hurt, and I let out a scream. I hastily retreated from the glass box, and in my moment of fear, I uttered words I'd rather not repeat, followed by a fervent declaration: "I never want to step on that thing again!"

The Burj Khalifa and the Willis Tower stand as remarkable achievements, among the greatest accomplishments in human history. The mere concept of constructing structures that soar over fourteen hundred feet into the sky is nothing short of awe-inspiring. These skyscrapers showcase unparalleled craftsmanship, and when considering other remarkable inventions, only a handful can rival the coolness of these architectural marvels.

When reflecting on extraordinary feats, it's essential to acknowledge an unparalleled work that dates back over two thousand years, one that remains the most profound act of selflessness and love ever undertaken. This work was carried out on the cross by Jesus Christ, an act of unparalleled sacrifice, where He willingly laid down His life to atone for our sins. His ultimate goal was to reconcile us with God, our loving Father, embodying the epitome of love and devotion.

SEPARATION

When God crafted the world, He bestowed upon humanity a precious gift—freewill, granting us the freedom to shape our own destinies. This gift endures to this day. I find great satisfaction in possessing freewill, yet there are moments when I yearn for clear guidance. However, with the gift of free will comes a perilous companion—sin. Your perception of sin may differ, but let's adopt a common understanding for the purpose of our discussion: sin is separation from God. In essence, sin represents the chasm between us and our Creator, the dwelling place of condemnation, shame, and guilt. The enemy cunningly exploits our freedom of choice, often steering it toward selfish ends.

Reflecting on the creation of the world, we witness a time of perfect harmony between humans and God. The book of Genesis beautifully depicts this idyllic state:

Adam and his wife were both naked, and they felt no shame. (Genesis 2:25 NIV)

Imagine that for a moment—nakedness without shame, a time and place where shame didn't exist. When harm, guilt, or sin didn't exist. It truly sounds marvelous! One can only envision the profound peace that enveloped those early moments. The enemy, who harbors a profound animosity toward us and God, is relentless in his pursuit of causing destruction to all that God cherishes. It is essential to grasp that, for some of you, this book will serve as an eye-opener, unveiling the cunning schemes the enemy employs in your life and equipping you with the knowledge to counter his actions.

For others, this book will be your first introduction to the concept of spiritual warfare. It is a very real battle that we engage in daily, all because of the following:

God had instructed Adam and Eve not to partake of the fruit from a specific tree within the garden they called home. They were free to enjoy the fruits of any other tree in the garden except for that one. Consider what transpired:

> When the woman saw that the fruit of the tree was good for food and pleasing to the eye, and also desirable for gaining wisdom, she took some and ate it. She also gave some to her husband, who was with her, and he ate it. (Genesis 3:6 NIV)

The idyllic, shame-free, guilt-free existence they once enjoyed was suddenly shattered, as evidenced by the following:

> But the Lord God called to the man, "Where are you?"

> He answered, "I heard you in the garden, and I was afraid because I was naked; so I hid." (Genesis 3:9-10 NIV)

Furthermore, the Lord God questioned the woman, who replied, "The serpent deceived me, and I ate," (Genesis 3:13 NIV). God had explicitly warned them against eating from that particular tree, and what did the enemy do? He disrupted the peace and harmony that prevailed. Adam and Eve weren't engaging in a game of hide-and-seek with God; they were hiding because they knew they had sinned. They felt shame for the first time in their lives. These are the first moments where shame entered humanity. The root of shame here is directly tied to disobedience to God. This seemingly small act of disobedience was the entry point for sin into the world.

Strikingly, we find ourselves doing the very same thing today. It's no different. We make regrettable choices, and once we've sinned, we often assume that God is furious with us, out to condemn us. Consequently, we tend to run away from God, seeking to conceal ourselves in the shadow of guilt and shame.

I recently had a conversation with a gentleman at a restaurant, and as I shared details about the church I attend, he confided, "I can't step into a church. If I do, it will crumble to the ground because of my past actions." Such sentiments reflect a common misconception. The enemy manipulates our thoughts, convincing us that God will unleash His wrath upon us, that our sins are too great to be reconciled by God's goodness. What we face is a separation issue that requires resolving.

RECONCILIATION

When I first met Allison, it didn't take me long to realize that I loved her deeply. My feelings for her were strong and unwavering, and I was convinced of it from the very beginning. However, Allison had a different perspective; she needed time to understand her own feelings. Out of my profound love for her, I was more than willing to give her the space and time she needed for her feelings to catch up to mine. It was after about a year and a few months of knowing her that I made a significant decision. I felt that it was the right moment to purchase an engagement ring for her.

I was filled with immense excitement at the thought of finding the perfect ring and presenting it to her, knowing it would bring a smile to her face. The idea of being able to do something so special for Allison warmed my heart. However, that excitement was short-lived when I discovered the price tag attached to the rings I liked. I began my search for the perfect ring, only to realize that rings could be quite expensive.

I found several options that were priced at thousands and thousands of dollars, far beyond my modest budget for a wedding ring. This led me to ponder, "How on earth could I afford something like this?" At one point, I even toyed with the idea of a simpler gesture, akin to what Derrick Shepherd and Meredith Grey did on Grey's Anatomy—expressing our love on a sticky note and framing it as a token of our commitment.

Deep down, I knew that such a gesture wouldn't suffice, so I continued my quest for the perfect ring. That's when I had the pleasure of meeting Les, a knowledgeable woman working at a jewelry store in a nearby mall.

Les was an absolute gem herself, offering invaluable assistance in my search. She introduced me to a ring known as the "princess cut," and it immediately captured my heart. It resembled a ring that Allison had shown me previously, and, interestingly, my affectionate nickname for her was "princess."

Curious about the price, I asked Les, and her response exceeded a thousand dollars. My heart sank as I contemplated how to make this work financially. I decided to take a look at my bank account, calculate my savings, and arrive at a conclusion. The ring was undeniably expensive, the most substantial purchase I had ever made other than buying a car. Yet, my love for Allison far surpassed any monetary sacrifice. Without hesitation, I handed over the money because, in my eyes, Allison was worth every single penny.

In August of 2017, I had the pleasure of giving Allison the princess cut ring, and her joy was palpable. I had planned a whimsical scavenger hunt for her, with clues leading her closer to me and the ring at the end. It was an adorable and memorable moment. The final clue was "keeper of my heart," a reference to a well-known statue in Wichita called "keeper of the plains," guiding her to my location.

The same way I had contemplated the expense of that ring and willingly paid the price for the one I loved, I couldn't help but draw a parallel to how God views each one of us. We are His beloved children, and despite any separation, His longing to be with us remains unwavering.

Sin is expensive and is responsible for separation from God. Who would bear the price tag, and what would it cost? God undertook the expense, but it certainly wasn't a small sum for Him. Can you fathom having to purchase your own children? The separation was the barrier that kept us distant from God. The only means to connect us with Him was to have something in between. That something was a sacrifice, a method to make amends for sin, a way to seek forgiveness for our wrongs, and a means to settle our debts in full.

This is the situation we find ourselves in until we embrace Jesus: In this predicament, we stand separated from God, unable to bridge the gap on our own. The solution, however, lies in the sacrificial act of Jesus. He is the bridge between our sinful state and God's righteousness. Through

Him, we find forgiveness for our wrongdoings and a way to settle the debt of our sins.

Imagine the immense love it took for God to send His own Son, Jesus, as the ultimate sacrifice to redeem us. It was a costly act, a divine gesture that reflects the depth of His love for humanity. Here is an image that depicts what our state is without a sacrifice for our wrongdoing.

God desires the same harmonious relationship with us that He once shared with Adam and Eve before sin entered the world. This is where Jesus enters the picture. Jesus, the Son of God, was sent because God recognized our need for a path back to Him. God understood that, without the shedding of blood to atone for sin, there would be no other means for us to reunite with Him, as death is the penalty for sin.

In the words of John 3:16 from the NIV Bible: "For God so loved the world that he gave his one and only Son, that whoever believes in him shall not perish but have eternal life."

At some point, our lives will conclude, and we will face our mortality. Death will be the culmination of our existence, and it will be our own life-blood that settles the score for our wrongdoings, or it will be Jesus's blood. Either way, someone is paying for our sin.

Jesus was well aware of what awaited Him, and He comprehended the purpose behind God's decision to send Him to earth: to live a flawless life on our behalf and ultimately offer Himself as the perfect sacrifice, allowing us to be reconciled with God. When faced with the prospect of enduring death, Jesus uttered these words: "Father, if you are willing, take this cup from me; yet not my will, but yours be done," (Matthew 22:42 NIV).

It's entirely understandable that Jesus sought an alternative to the excruciating death on the cross that lay before Him. Nevertheless, He recognized that there was no other viable option; someone had to atone for the world's multitude of wrongs, and He willingly accepted this responsibility.

In Philippians 2:5-9 (NIV), we read: "Let this mind be in you which was also in Christ Jesus, who, being in the form of God, did not consider it robbery to be equal with God, but made Himself of no reputation, taking the form of a bondservant, and coming in the likeness of men. And being found in appearance as a man, He humbled Himself and became obedient to the point of death, even the death on the cross. Therefore, God also has highly exalted Him and given Him the name which is above every name."

God's profound love for the world compelled Him to send His Son, Jesus, as the bridge that would restore our connection with Him. Jesus lived a life that was both entirely human and fully divine, demonstrating humility and perfection on our behalf. He willingly endured a death that was meant for us, thereby paving a way to close the gap that separated us from God.

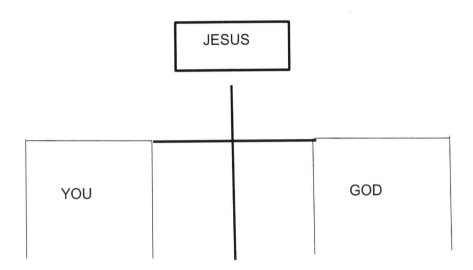

God's love is incredibly valuable, and He willingly paid a high price for your sake. The sacrifice was so worthwhile to Him because it meant having you in His embrace. It's essential to realize that God's love is not just a simple, ordinary affection. It's a love so deep, so profound, that it cost Him dearly. But He didn't hesitate for a moment, for the joy of having you in His life made it all worth it.

You see, God's love isn't something that can be measured in material terms. It's not about gold or silver, but about the immeasurable worth He places on you. His love is a treasure beyond compare, and He gave everything to have you by His side. So, my dear friend, remember this truth and hold it close to your heart: God's love is priceless, and you are the precious reason why He paid such a high price.

SALVATION

The gift of life bestowed upon us is known as salvation, a precious offering freely given through the sacrifice of Jesus. It's not merely a ticket to heaven upon our demise, but it's also about reuniting with God as His cherished children. You, dear reader, are a son or daughter of the Almighty, and He yearns to play an active role in your life, just like a loving father. As we discussed in the preceding chapter, His love for you knows no bounds; He desires nothing less than the very best for you!

Life to the fullest starts with Jesus.

When you embrace Jesus as your Lord and Savior, you receive this invaluable gift of salvation. It ensures not only your place in heaven but also the constant presence of a Father who will walk beside you throughout your journey on this earth. I'm reminded of the profound words Jesus spoke during His earthly ministry, expressing His purpose:

The thief comes only to steal and kill and destroy; I have come that they may have life, and have it to the full. (John 10:10 NIV)

This verse serves as the inspiration for the title of this book. True fulfillment can only be found in Jesus. Life to the fullest starts with Jesus. He yearns to quench the thirst of your soul and cleanse it anew.

I once had the privilege of leading a young man to Jesus, sharing the same message I'm presenting to you now. After he accepted Jesus into his heart, I asked him, "How do you feel?" His response was heartfelt: "Loved and cared for. It's as if the weight of the world has been lifted from my shoulders." I desire that same experience for you. I've poured my time and energy into creating this book because I genuinely believe that this is the path to a life truly lived to the fullest. This life can be yours; will you accept the precious gift of salvation?

In the upcoming chapter, we will explore what it means to embrace this priceless gift of salvation.

MOMENT OF REFLECTION

- What thoughts came to mind when reading about the root of shame?

- What were your preconceived notions about Jesus before this chapter?

- Have you seen yourself in need of a perfect Savior?

- Have you ever paid for something expensive? How did it make you feel?

- Did this chapter ignite a spark within your heart?

- If you have already accepted Jesus, how did this chapter resonate with your own journey?

ACCEPTING THE SAVIOR

My wife, Allison, once faced a challenging decision, and I keenly observed her choice. The situation unfolded when she made a somewhat unkind remark about a friend. I genuinely believe she didn't intend to be hurtful; rather, she was expressing her opinion she had about what her friend was doing. Well, what Allison said made it back to her friend who then made it known that they didn't want to be friends anymore.

When I saw Allison's face after she found out her friend had heard her words about them, Allison was devastated. She was in tears. I could tell she genuinely felt hurt that her friend felt hurt. My heart ached for her.

In that moment, I offered my encouragement and comfort, asking her what she believed was the right course of action. Allison, bravely suggested that the right thing to do was to visit her friend in person, knock on their door, and apologize face-to-face.

Summoning great courage, Allison decided to go and apologize. This decision was far from easy, and I deeply admire her for it. It revealed a remarkable aspect of her character.

We all occasionally say things we don't truly mean. The majority of people in the world are also not seeking out relational conflict. In fact, many do whatever possible to avoid it. This conflict can happen so unintentionally like with Allison's case.

Likewise, you may have unintentionally said something hurtful to someone at some point. Deciding what to say and when to say it can be challenging, but life presents us with even more emotionally charged decisions. From choosing our attire and where to live to deciding on purchases and birthday gifts, life confronts us with significant choices. We ponder which school or college to attend, which career path to follow, and even how to recognize the right person for a relationship. Car choices, maintaining friendships, and planning for retirement all demand careful consideration.

These decisions carry substantial weight and significance. Life is full of choices, ranging from situations similar to Allison's to the ones that simply come with growing up. I read in a book one time that "life is simply a combination of all the choices we have made."

In my experience some of the most difficult choices are in regard to relationships. Those are the choices that seem to carry the most weight. Whether it's a friendship, a conflict with someone, or dating relationship, relational related choices carry significant weight.

There is one relationship decision that stands as the single most important choice we will ever make—the decision with immense weight and significance. It's a decision that all of us will ultimately face someday: our decision regarding a relationship with Jesus Christ.

In a previous part of this book, I shared my journey to NewSpring and how I encountered Jesus in a way that was entirely new to me. It was an experience that allowed me to understand Jesus's love for me in a profoundly different light than I had ever heard before. I came to understand that He loved me deeply, cared for me genuinely, and desired a personal relationship with me. This realization was a pivotal moment, as I recognized that I lacked a genuine relationship with Him. It was a realization that demanded action because a genuine relationship is inherently personal, and Jesus was becoming increasingly personal to me.

This is exactly what Jesus intended. He longed for a personal connection with me, for me to understand authentically what my sin represented and how He took my place. I previously mentioned how I began to feel His love pursuing me, as if it were calling my name every single day.

One Sunday at church, someone shared about that stirring feeling in my heart. It was like the preacher was talking to only me. That person said "You have to respond to the love God is trying to show you. Either accept Him or run from Him."

What's remarkable about God is that He never imposes His will upon us. On that day, I had the option to continue running, to persist in ignoring that burning sensation in my heart. Perhaps, with time, it might have faded away. But one thing was abundantly clear—the choice was mine to make. I fully grasped that God had chosen me, but the question loomed: Would I choose Him?

THE ROOM

I recall one late night in September of 2013, at the age of eighteen, I found myself in my room at home, my heart filled with questions and a longing. I couldn't shake off the thoughts that had lingered since my last visit to church. The message had been clear—the choice was mine, and God was ready to embrace me as His child.

Uncertain about what to do, I recalled the advice from church: just talk to Jesus and He'll meet you right there. So, not knowing what else to do, I knelt down in my upstairs bedroom. As soon as I knelt and focused all of my thoughts on Jesus, I began to cry as love overwhelmed my heart.

With trembling words and tears streaming down my face, I reached out to Jesus. It wasn't a perfectly composed prayer by any means, but that's the beauty of Jesus—He doesn't demand perfection; He simply desires us.

Kneeling there, I cried as I conversed with Jesus. I questioned Him, wondering why He would love me so intensely when I felt undeserving of such love. The love in my heart only intensified as I asked Him, "Why me? Why did You go to such lengths to seek me out?"

In tears, overwhelmed by His love and grace, I uttered a heartfelt plea. I begged Jesus to enter my heart and my life, to save me, to usher in a new beginning. I yearned for the profound love that had begun to blossom within my heart to cleanse my soul and to provide me with satisfaction and a fresh start.

I needed a Savior, and I was fully aware of it at that moment. My sin was so real to me and there was no other way to overcome it besides Jesus.

It was in that very room that Jesus met me, and my life underwent a transformation that would endure forever. I'll share the details of the prayer and the remarkable events that followed, but first, let me share a story from the Bible—a story of a woman who just wanted something to drink. I believe we can all relate to her story.

THE WELL

One day, Jesus embarked on a journey from the southern region of Judea to the northern expanse of Galilee, known as northern Israel today. While the swiftest route would have led him through Samaria, a challenge loomed before him. In the context of Jesus's time, a significant cultural divide existed between Jews and Samaritans. This divide was so pronounced that Jews typically avoided any association with Samaritans. Consequently, when Jews journeyed from Judea to Galilee, instead of traversing the direct path through Samaria, they would detour around it, bypassing the Samaritan territory.

Have you ever experienced the feeling of being passed over or overlooked? It brings to mind a memory from my middle school days when I eagerly decided to try out for the school basketball team. I was confident that I would make it onto the team! Following a grueling week of intense conditioning (which means run until you can't run any more), the coach posted the list of those who had earned a spot on the team and those who hadn't. The list was prominently displayed in the school's central hallway for all to see.

The morning after the tryouts, I approached the list with excitement, hoping to find my name among the chosen few. A cluster of fellow students surrounded the list, eagerly checking the results. As I scanned the names, I spotted a few of my friends who had made the team, and I couldn't help but feel genuinely happy for them. It meant I would be playing alongside them, after all. However, as I continued to scan the list, I realized that my name was nowhere to be found. It wasn't there, not even a trace of it. I felt a wave of embarrassment come over me, and I couldn't bear to be around my friends that day.

In that moment, I felt bypassed. Perhaps you've encountered a similar experience, whether at work, in a relationship, or even during your school days. The sting of being bypassed leaves a profound sense of discomfort and brings a world of questions.

Jesus knew all about someone that had felt bypassed. He faced a choice: would He adhere to convention and bypass Samaria like everyone else, or would He chart a different course? When the time came for Jesus to make His decision, He opted to defy the norm.

Rather than avoiding Samaria, he chose to traverse it, stepping into the very place where tradition dictated he shouldn't go. In this act, Jesus challenged societal expectations and showed us the importance of breaking free from preconceived boundaries. His decision to go through Samaria serves as a profound reminder that, sometimes, choosing the unconventional path can lead to unexpected and transformative experiences.

He deliberately immersed himself in a culture different from his own Jewish heritage, refusing to bypass Samaria. This decision raised questions among those who followed him. Would they be angered by his choice? Would they consider it a betrayal?

What sets Jesus apart is his intentionality; he possesses an innate understanding of our needs and is willing to go to great lengths to meet us where we are. Jesus's actions always have a purpose. Let's dive into the intriguing beginning of this narrative:

He had to go through Samaria on the way. Eventually he came to the Samaritan village of Sychar, near the field that Jacob gave to his son Joseph. Jacob's well was there; and Jesus, tired from the long walk, sat wearily beside the well about noontime (John 4:4-6 NLT).

One can't help but wonder about Jesus's thoughts as he embarked on this less-traveled road. Perhaps he was drawn by the prospect of quenching his thirst at the well. Maybe he sought a shorter route. It's conceivable that he simply wished to observe what might unfold, or perhaps, he harbored the belief that a greater purpose awaited him. Take a look at this map, which reveals the landscape and route that Jesus walked during that era:

The path Jesus chose, leading directly from Jerusalem to Nazareth, wound through the heart of Samaria. In contrast, the route most commonly taken by Jews curved out and around to the right, deliberately avoiding this region.

One thing that truly sets Jesus apart is his fearlessness in the face of societal norms and expectations. He paid no heed to what others might think of him or his choices. A Jew opting to journey through Samaria? In the cultural context of the time, that was nearly unimaginable!

To put it in perspective, the distance from where he began his journey to Sychar was roughly thirty-one miles. That's a considerable distance to cover, especially in the scorching heat of the Middle Eastern desert. Now, let's get into what unfolds next in this remarkable story:

Soon a Samaritan woman came to draw water, and Jesus said to her, "Please give me a drink." He was alone at the time because his disciples had gone into the village to buy some food. (John 4:7-8 NLT)

As Jesus sat there, a Samaritan woman approached him. At this point in the story, we know little about her. Her name and her life's story remain a mystery. However, what we do know is that Jesus, weary from his journey, found himself engaging in a conversation with her. While the narrative doesn't provide a name for the Samaritan woman, let's call her Emma from here onward. Let's find out what Emma had to say to Jesus when she encountered him at the well.

The woman (Emma) was surprised, for Jews refuse to have anything to do with Samaritans. She said to Jesus, "You are a Jew, and I am a Samaritan woman. Why are you asking me for a drink?" (John 4:9 NLT)

Emma couldn't fathom why a Jewish man, Jesus, would dare to have a conversation with her, a Samaritan. Can you imagine the perplexed expression on Emma's face? Jesus had shattered the cultural boundaries that had defined her entire life, and she couldn't help but wonder why.

Emma might have felt a mix of emotions—embarrassment, confusion, maybe even a touch of fear. What if someone spotted her talking with Jesus? What would they say? Emma had long been the one bypassed by others, but now, in this encounter, everything was about to change.

Jesus replied, "If you only knew the gift God has for you and who you are speaking to, you would ask me, and I would give you living water." "But sir, you don't have a rope or a bucket," she said, "and this well is very deep. Where would you get this living water? And besides, do you think you're greater than our ancestor Jacob, who gave us this well? How can you offer better water than he and his sons and his animals enjoyed?" (John 4:10-12 NLT)

Emma wondered, "What water is he talking about, and where could it possibly come from?" Emma noticed that Jesus lacked the tools for drawing water—no bucket, no rope, nothing. Emma did what we naturally do, her mind went straight to the resources. Emma, in essence, was questioning herself, who is this man, and what in the world is He talking about? He doesn't have the right resources to draw water. And living water, what is that? I've never heard of such a thing! Perhaps he's been out in the sun for too long!

It was a valid point; after all, they were both in the midst of a scorching desert, and Jesus had no means to draw water. Emma was thinking logically, and Jesus proceeded to address her concerns.

Jesus replied, "Anyone who drinks this water will soon become thirsty again. But those who drink the water I give will never be thirsty again. It becomes a fresh, bubbling spring within them, giving them eternal life" (John 4:13-14 NLT).

Jesus acknowledged Emma's skepticism by explaining that drinking from the well would leave her thirsty again. I love how Jesus is kind to her by speaking to her logic. He then conveyed to her, in terms she could grasp, how He could give her a new and abundant life.

Perhaps, in the grand scheme of things, Jesus did have a purpose for traveling through Samaria. Perhaps He foresaw that Emma would visit the well that day, seeking a drink. Maybe He knew that Emma needed Him, even if she hadn't realized it herself.

All along, Emma had been fixated on quenching her physical thirst, while Jesus was offering her something far greater—the concept of living water. Once Jesus made it clear that He possessed this living water, which, if consumed, would quench her thirst forever, Emma reacted in the way any of us would!

"Please, sir," the woman (Emma) said, "give me this water! Then I'll never be thirsty again, and I won't have to come here to get water." (John 4:15 NLT)

Emma's gaze met Jesus's, and she boldly exclaimed with a voice filled with longing, "Give me this water, now!" If someone offered us such a promise, we'd all be clamoring for that life-changing water, wouldn't we? Water that could make the pains of life go away? Water that could make the suffering go away? Water that would make the tough realities of life disappear?

This whole scenario brings to mind a memorable commercial from a company called J.G. Wentworth. In those ads, someone desperately in need of money passionately cries out, "It's my money, and I need it now!" Emma's fervent plea feels much the same: "It's my water, and I need it now!"

What happens next in this encounter between Emma and Jesus is quite extraordinary. Emma had demanded this mysterious water from Jesus, and

He responds with a surprising request: "Go and get your husband," He tells her. Emma, somewhat puzzled, replies, "I don't have a husband" (John 4:16-17a NLT).

At this point, Emma probably thought, "What does my marital status have to do with receiving water?" Little did she know that she was in for an even bigger surprise. Jesus reveals her past in a way that must have left her stunned:

"You're right! You don't have a husband—for you have had five husbands, and you aren't even married to the man you're living with now. You certainly spoke the truth!" (John 4:17b-18 NLT).

Wow! Can you imagine the shock Emma felt? If I were in her shoes, I might drop my watering bucket and run for the hills! I cannot imagine the look on Emma's face when Jesus says this to her. Could you imagine someone coming up to you sharing your sin with you? How would you react if someone suddenly confronted you with your own misdeeds? I know I'd probably feel pretty defeated.

As Jesus laid bare her past, Emma must have wondered, "How does He know all this about me?" Her expression likely shifted to one of shame, and she might have thought Jesus had heard it through gossip or that there was something supernatural about the water He possessed. With a heavy heart, Emma probably muttered to herself, "I don't know how this man knows about my past relationships. I'm disappointed in myself."

Yet, there they stood, in the scorching heat of the day, beside that well. Emma, now looking up at Jesus, quietly says "I see you are a prophet." By now, she realized that Jesus was no ordinary man. She probably thought about how she wished Jesus would have bypassed Samaria like everyone else after He brought this up.

Emma, standing there with so many questions, wondering what is happening, remembers she has heard about a man called the Messiah. Emma tells Jesus she knows that a man called Messiah will come one day, and this is what happens next:

"I do know that the Messiah is coming. When he arrives, we'll get the whole story."

"I am he," said Jesus. "You don't have to wait any longer or look any further." Just then, his disciples came back. They were shocked. They couldn't believe he was talking with that kind of a woman. No one said what they were all thinking, but their faces showed it (John 4:25b-27 MSG).

The disciples were shocked to see Jesus talking with Emma, but they didn't know Emma's story. They didn't know Jesus went through Samaria just to meet Emma that day.

Emma woke up that morning just like she always did to get water. Only this day was different. Emma showed up at that well and met Jesus. Jesus cut through the red tape of culture just to meet with her. Jesus chose Emma long before Emma ever chose Jesus.

I love Jesus; he didn't care about the opinions of others. He couldn't have cared less about that! He cared about Emma's heart and what she was going through more than anything. I know the story didn't mention it, but you know she had to have been carrying baggage associated with guilt from how she was living. That's what Jesus cared about, and He cared about the fact that Emma needed love, peace, and forgiveness. Emma needed life to the fullest.

There's a song that fits this story perfectly by a lady named Olivia Lane called "Woman At The Well," which shares Emma's experience in the form of song. Some of the lyrics go like this:

Tonight I feel just like the woman at the well...Wonderin' how someone could love me, when I can't love myself. But you want me as I am and that sounds crazy. I guess maybe that's why grace is so amazing. It's no longer just a story when I read it. Cause I've seen Him for myself and I believe it.

The words Jesus spoke to Emma when he perfectly married truth and grace, "you don't have to wait any longer or look any further," hold true for each one of us. There's no need to continue searching for fulfillment endlessly. You won't discover it by pursuing a career, accumulating material or financial wealth, relying on alcohol or drugs, or seeking popularity and influence. The kind of success gained through these means is fleeting, and I assure you, the high it brings always fades away.

A dear friend of mine, who used drugs in the past to numb his pain, once confided in me, saying, "I've tried all sorts of drugs to find that high and numbness, but nothing, I mean absolutely nothing, compares to the fulfillment and high I've found in Jesus."

Jesus wants for you what He wanted for Emma. A life to the fullest that can only be experienced through Him. Salvation through Jesus is open to everyone, without exception. It's not limited to a select few. The Gospel doesn't care about your income, the car you drive, your fashion choices, or your address. What truly matters is the state of your heart.

I've witnessed young children recognizing their need for Jesus in their lives, seeking His salvation, and being baptized. It's truly astonishing. I've seen countless middle school, high school, and college students who have raised their hands and earnestly asked Jesus to transform them into pure individuals who seek the Kingdom of Heaven.

I recall a heartwarming moment during a summer camp when a middle school student was in tears, overwhelmed by the love he felt from Jesus that day during the message I had just finished preaching. Jesus had been chasing him down. He prayed for salvation, and that very night, I had the privilege of baptizing him in a local swimming pool.

In a church service one day, I'll never forget an elderly man, likely in his nineties, who could barely walk. Despite his frailty, raised his hand to accept Jesus and slowly made his way down the aisle to the front of the room, tears streaming down his face.

Nothing can compare to the lasting fulfillment that Jesus offers. He provides enduring peace and comfort and will never abandon you. He'll stand with you through the fires of life, regardless of the baggage you carry. He wants you just as you are, just as He did Emma.

Just as Jesus chose Emma, He chooses you. There's no need to wait any longer or search any further. The promise of a full and meaningful life is available to you today. Jesus's words from the Bible hold true for you right now:

You did not choose me, but I chose you. (John 15:16a, NIV)

Jesus chooses you, and He understands your past. He's aware of how you feel and what you've done, yet He still desires you. Jesus longs to shower you with grace and a love that surpasses any you've ever known.

Jesus chose you before you chose Him.

Jesus chased me down and met me that September night in my room. He went out of His way, paying no attention to society, and met Emma at the well on that scorching day as she sought water.

Just as He met me in my room and Emma by the well, He's ready to meet you where you are as well.

WHERE IS JESUS MEETING YOU?

In Jesus there is forgiveness and there is no condemnation. There is actually a freedom that exists! There is a life we can have that's not ridden with guilt and shame. A life that has purpose to it:

Therefore, there is now no condemnation for those who are in Christ Jesus. (Romans 8:1 NIV)

To accept Jesus, scripture tells us how:

If you declare with your mouth, "Jesus is Lord," and believe that God raised him from the dead, you will be saved. For it is with your heart that you believe and are justified, and it is with your mouth that you profess your faith and are saved. (Romans 10:9-10 NIV)

Wherever you are and whatever you are doing, I invite you to pray this prayer just like I did that September night in my room. Embrace the feeling of Jesus tugging at your heart. Today is the day. Not tomorrow, not next week or not in two months or two years:

Jesus, I confess that I am a sinner. Please save me. Jesus, I surrender my life to you. Come into my heart and come into my life. I make you my Lord and Savior. Forgive me, Jesus. Give me life to the fullest in you. Amen.

If you prayed that prayer for the first time, congratulations! I'm absolutely thrilled about the decision you've just made! If I were with you right now, I'd give you the biggest hug. Your life with Jesus is about to take on a whole new dimension. You've embraced a new identity and a fresh purpose in life, and it's going to be an exciting journey ahead. Over the next two sections of this book, we'll dive into what this new life means for you from this point onward. We'll discuss the significance of your new identity, the power of prayer, and what it truly means to live with and for Jesus.

Now, if you've experienced salvation before, I encourage you to keep reading. There's something valuable for you in the upcoming pages. You never know how Jesus might touch your heart through the insights we're about to explore.

MOMENT OF REFLECTION

- For those who've encountered salvation prior to reading this book, what memories has this book stirred within you regarding your own journey of salvation? How can you use these memories as moments of reflection and gratitude?

- If you prayed that powerful prayer for the first time today, once again, congratulations! I encourage you to grab a journal, a piece of paper, phone or in a page on this book and note down today's date, so it remains etched in your memory. Write down what you're thinking and feeling right now so you can go back to it later.

- Take a moment to pause and reflect. As you do, listen to Olivia Lane's song, "Woman at the Well," to further connect with your emotions?

- I would love to hear from you. I want to know your story and how Jesus is speaking to you right now. Feel free to send me an email and share how this book has impacted you thus far. Perhaps it's rekindled memories, revealed new insights, or even allowed you to encounter Jesus in a profound way today. Whatever it may be, I'm here to listen and support you every step of the way. You can also find other ways to connect with me on the connect page at the end of this book.

    Email me at: bryant@bryantwestbrook.com

PART 2:

LIFE WITH

THE SAVIOR

KNOWING YOUR IDENTITY

At the age of 19, right after graduating from high school, my journey with Jesus kicked off. I was brimming with zeal for Jesus and that enthusiasm didn't go unnoticed. It was during this time that a friend of mine approached me with a brand-new and unique proposition: Would I be interested in speaking at our local middle school's Fellowship Of Christian Athletes gathering. I pondered this new opportunity for a while.

The essence of FCA, with its focus on setting aside time for prayer within the school day, struck me as a fantastic idea. As my friend shared more details about the new opportunity to speak at FCA, I found myself increasingly intrigued.

You see, I had never stood before a crowd and delivered a presentation before—not once in my life. Nevertheless, I agreed to take on the challenge, knowing that I could choose any topic to preach about.

Questions swirled in my mind. What do middle schoolers yearn to know? What should they know? What if I falter? Would I ever get another opportunity like this? I devoted an astonishing thirty hours too many to prepare for what was essentially a seven-minute speech. I rehearsed tirelessly, even recording myself delivering the sermon for practice. Looking back at that video today, I'm struck by two emotions: first, my deep admiration for my passion for God's word, and secondly, sheer amazement that they had invited me to speak!

The fateful day eventually arrived, and as I walked into the classroom, my nerves were palpable—I was trembling! Inside the room, a teacher instructed me to place my Bible on a music stand set up in front of the class I was about to address. However, I couldn't help but notice that this particular music stand was piled high with an enormous stack of papers. I knew I had to be extra cautious.

Approaching the stand, I gingerly placed my Bible on it, and what unfolded next was unexpected. Every single piece of paper, including my Bible, toppled off that tiny music stand! Papers were strewn everywhere, and the entire middle school audience burst into laughter.

Embarrassment flooded over me, and I attempted to retrieve the scattered papers. There were just so many of them—hundreds! With the class out of control at the expense of my amusement, finally, the teacher intervened by looking at me and saying, "Just please start talking and pick this up after class because we're about to run out of time here."

Despite the huge mess I made, I summoned the courage of a raindrop and was able to share from the Bible. That day, sixteen kids raised their hands, expressing their desire to live their lives for Jesus. It's a memory I'll cherish forever. Besides making a fool of myself, I learned a valuable lesson—I don't have to chase perfection, I just have to be available.

Jesus can use my best efforts, even if they fall short of perfection or lead to failure. That day, I gave it my all, far from perfect, yet, He still used my words to touch those kids. As for whether the school invited me back to speak again, well, they didn't. Nine years have passed, and I'm still awaiting that elusive invitation.

Much like the new experience I had when speaking at the FCA, I encountered something profoundly new when I began my relationship with Jesus.

I remember the shift after Jesus saved me; I felt like a different person. Not a perfect person, but different. Something had changed within me. I experienced a profound sense of belonging and a deep love in my heart and soul. I was filled a fresh zeal for Jesus and for life. I had taken on a new identity. I knew, without a shadow of a doubt, that something remarkable had occurred, and I yearned to learn more.

Chances are, you've felt this too. Whether it was when you first accepted Jesus as your Savior years ago or as you read this book, those feelings you're experiencing are real, and you shouldn't discount them.

YOU ARE A NEW CREATION

The moment you asked and accepted Jesus into your heart, something incredible happened. You took on a new form of you. Your identity underwent a transformation. Who you are changed, and you embraced a new version of yourself.

You are now living as someone approved by God and deeply loved by Him. In God's eyes, you are a new creation. He sees that you've entrusted your life to Jesus, and you no longer carry the weight of your sins.

One of my favorite verses in the entire Bible is 2 Corinthians 5:17 because it beautifully encapsulates our identity in Christ after salvation. This scripture is the foundation upon which we can build a fulfilling life:

"Therefore, if anyone is in Christ, the new creation has come: The old has gone, the new is here! (2 Corinthians 5:17 NIV)

This verse signifies the beginning of a fresh chapter in your life. It's like having a second birthday, embarking on a new journey, and realizing that you've shed your old self. You are now on a completely new path, with Jesus as your savior. But what does "the old" really mean? It doesn't refer to your interests in life, such as your hobbies, creativity, earthly family, or job. That's part of who you are. These things matter, and God cares about them. While God might guide you regarding these aspects of your life, they aren't what "the old" represents. Pick up your cross and deny yourself doesn't mean deny yourself of the good things that you love.

"The old" pertains to who you were on the inside.

In the past, your inner self was all about you. Frankly, you were the center of your universe. You determined your self-worth and chased after fleeting pleasures because you hadn't experienced the new life yet. You sought approval relentlessly but never truly found it anywhere. All of these and much more constitute "the old." It was like carrying baggage, dead weight that held you back. But now, God has brought about a profound change in your life.

NO LONGER A FOREIGNER, BUT A CHILD

Accepting Jesus as your savior means much more than securing your spot in heaven; it's about becoming part of a loving family. You're not just any family member; you're now a cherished child of God. I recall a wise Bible teacher advising me to see myself as a "loved child of God" after my salvation, for that's precisely who I had become. This Bible teacher actually had us do an exercise where we practiced saying this to others. Our partner would say, "Hi, my name is ____, who are you? We would respond with "loved child of God."

Repeating this exercise many times over help me grasp just how my new identity was. This meant that before anything else in my life, I was a loved child of God.

That's who you are too—loved, valued, and cherished by your heavenly Father. It's terrific news because you've got a heavenly Father who deeply cares for you. The book of Galatians in the Bible beautifully illustrates this concept and clarifies what it means to be loved by God:

So in Christ Jesus you are all children of God through faith. (Galatians 3:26 NIV)

But when the set time had fully come, God sent his son, born of a woman, born under the law, that we might receive adoption to sonship. Because you are his sons, God sent the Spirit of his son into our hearts, the Spirit who calls out, "Abba, Father." So you are no longer a slave, but God's child; and since you are his child, God has made you also an heir. (Galatians 4:4-7 NIV)

The term "adoption" carries powerful symbolism. Adoption is significant because it is the act of welcoming a new family member with open arms, seeing the other person in your mind as one of you now and that nothing could change that.

Think back to those times when you visited a friend's house. When you got hungry or thirsty, you politely asked if you could have something from their fridge. "Is it OK if I grab a snack from your fridge?" you'd ask. But when your friends visited your house, you didn't have to ask, it wasn't rude; it was your family's fridge, and in a way, it belonged to you.

Similarly, your membership in God's family carries with it a sense of belonging. As a child of God, you're part of this family, and nothing you do can remove you from it. You have a place here, and that place is yours forever.

YOU CANNOT LOSE YOUR PLACE IN THE FAMILY

In one of Jesus's stories, there was a father who owned a farm, and he had two sons. It was expected that these two sons would work on the farm and eventually take over its ownership, carrying on the family legacy. This farm was more than just a piece of land; it symbolized an inheritance and a significant milestone in the family's history. The older son diligently toiled on the farm, day in and day out. He never grumbled about the hard work, always keeping in mind that one day it would all belong to him. On the other hand, the younger son had a different idea. He wanted out, and he approached his father with a bold request.

The younger son said to his father, "Father, give me my share of the estate." And so, his father divided his property between them. Not long after that, the younger son gathered all his belongings, set off for a distant land, and squandered his wealth on a life of excess and recklessness (Luke 15:12-13 NIV).

Upon reading this, I couldn't help but wonder how the younger son mustered the courage to ask, or even demand, his father's share. And why did the father comply? The son got what he wanted and left, but the emotions on both sides were starkly different.

Imagine the son's happiness; he felt on top of the world. He was rich and finally free to live life his way, or so he believed. In contrast, the father likely felt a deep sense of betrayal and despair. He wasn't celebrating; he had lost a son. There might have been a tinge of shame too, as he knew where his hard-earned money would end up.

The son let his immediate desires overshadow his long-term vision. It's challenging to see how this could lead to a positive outcome, don't you think? Have you ever found yourself in a position similar to either the father or the son? Perhaps you're in the father's shoes, dealing with a child who's lost their way, making poor choices, and not showing respect. If that's you, you might feel lost, without answers, and even guilty for not guiding your child down the right path.

Alternatively, maybe you're the son in this story. You chose to disregard your parent or guardian's teachings and went your own way. Your attempts at living life on your terms might have led to regret and shame, not just for yourself but also for your family.

Sadly, the story takes a darker turn for the son. Eventually, he loses everything because he squandered it all on his own desires. Everything. Even though the money his dad gave him was substantial.

His pursuit of pleasure proved more insatiable than the wealth he had.

At this pivotal moment, he found himself at a crossroads, a standstill. The weight of his choices hung heavily over him, and he grappled with what to do next. Should he swallow his pride and return to his father, bearing the burden of squandering the family's wealth? Or should he persist in his current existence, tending to livestock, all the while sharing his meager meals and sleeping alongside the very pigs he had once cared for? This narrative serves as a powerful reminder of an enduring truth:

Sinful thoughts left unchecked lead to sinful actions.

Sinful thoughts start to pop up in our minds and when left unchecked or unquestioned, they start to lead to sinful desires which manifest as sinful actions. Sinful actions ultimately culminate in shame. It's a cycle that repeats itself relentlessly. If you had asked him about his future aspirations before he left his father's house, he would never have envisioned himself in this wretched state, dining with swine in utter disgrace. Yet, in his desperation, he made a momentous decision—to return home to his father.

He felt as though he had exhausted all other options to extricate himself from the abyss he had descended into. What would his father's reaction be? Surprisingly, it was filled with compassion and grace. Look at how Jesus shares the rest of the story:

> When he came to his senses, he said, "How many of my father's hired servants have food to spare, and here I am starving to death! I will set out and go back to my father and say to him: Father, I have sinned against heaven and against you. I am no longer worthy to be called your son; make me like one of your hired servants." So he got up and went to his father. But while he was still a long way off, his father saw him and was filled with compassion for him; he ran to his son, threw his arms around him and kissed him. The son said to him, "Father, I have sinned against heaven and against you. I am no longer worthy to be called your son." But the father said to his servants, "Quick! Bring the best robe and put it on him. Put a ring on his finger and sandals on his feet. Bring the fattened calf and kill it. Let's have a feast and celebrate. For this son of mine was dead and is alive again; he was lost and is found." So they began to celebrate." (Luke 15:17-22, NIV)

On that day, the father displayed an extraordinary, radical love for his son. He didn't sit idly, waiting for a sad speech or pleas for mercy. No, he sprinted toward his wayward child, his heart filled with longing to welcome him home. The remarkable aspect of this story lies in the father's awareness.

We previously established that the father wasn't foolish; he fully comprehended his son's intentions with his inheritance. Despite being aware of his son's misdeeds, his overwhelming love outweighed the son's transgressions. This exemplifies the power of love.

He threw the grandest celebration the farm had ever witnessed to mark the return of his younger son. Remarkably, the son's place in the family remained unaltered because the father's love surpassed any sinful mistakes.

Similar to the son's warm welcome home, you too are embraced by the father. Just as the son retained his position as a family member, so will you. God's love for you transcends any sinful errors you've committed.

You cannot lose your place in God's family.

The book of Romans provides assurance of our place in the family:

> And I am convinced that nothing can ever separate us from God's love. Neither death nor life, neither angels nor demons, neither our fears for today nor our worries about tomorrow—not even the powers of hell can separate us from God's love. No power in the sky above or in the earth below—indeed, nothing in all creation will ever be able to separate us from the love of God that is revealed in Christ Jesus our Lord. (Romans 3:38-39, NLT)

Your place in God's family is secure; you cannot lose it. Meaning, you cannot you're your salvation. It's secure. If somehow a wrong choice could take you out of God's family, then what Adam did earlier in this book would be greater than what Jesus did on the cross. My friend, that is simply not true. Through Jesus and His sacrifice on the cross for your sins, you have redemption. Jesus Himself assured us of this promise, recorded in the book of John:

> I give them eternal life, and they shall never perish; no one will snatch them out of my hand. (John 10:28, NIV)

No one and nothing can separate you from God's love once you accept Him as your savior. You are sealed into the family. I want to leave you with a promise from Jesus, deeply rooted in His identity even before His birth. It is written in the book of Matthew:

> The virgin will conceive and give birth to a son, and they will call him Immanuel (which means "God with us"). (Matthew 1:23, NIV)

Jesus's very name signifies His presence with us. May all of this bring you peace and comfort. I hope and pray that as you discover and are reminded of these truths, you feel God's presence in your heart, reaffirming your place in His family. Once again, once you accept Jesus as your Savior like we saw in the previous chapter, your place in God's family is secure.

MOMENT OF REFLECTION

- Let's wrap up this chapter by embarking on an exercise together. We're going to explore some Scriptures and do a little word switcheroo. Wherever you encounter "us" or "we," let's replace those pronouns with your name. Just for this exercise, I'm going to replace those with the name Emma, the woman from the well we talked about earlier in the book.

  For He chose us (Emma) in him before the creation of the world to be holy and blameless in his sight. In love he predestined us (Emma) for adoption to sonship through Jesus Christ, in accordance with his pleasure and will—to the praise of his glorious grace, which he has freely given us (Emma) in the One he loves. In him we (Emma has) have redemption through his blood, the forgiveness of sins, in accordance with the riches of God's grace that he lavished on us (Emma). (Ephesians 1:4-8 NIV)

- These words hold true not just for Emma but for you too. You are wrapped in God's grace and love. Jesus's sacrifice on the cross redeems you, and in God's eyes, you are spotless and part of His family. Remember, your newfound identity is "loved by God."

- You are a brand-new creation, and God desires for you to embrace your role in His family. Take a moment to reflect on the ideas we've discussed in this chapter, and how you've perceived yourself in the past.

- Consider these questions, and if you have a journal or something to jot down notes, use it to capture your thoughts for future reference:

  ➤ What has defined your sense of self in the past? This could be a hobby, a job, a sport, a school subject you excelled at, or anything you've tied your worth to.

  ➤ How have the Scriptures in this chapter transformed your self-perception? What does God's promise of never losing your place in His family mean to you personally?

  ➤ How will this newfound understanding impact your day-to-day life? Will what you've read affect the choices you make each day? Why or why not?

  ➤ What can you do daily to remind yourself that you have a cherished place in God's family?

  ➤ How can you daily reinforce your new identity as "loved by God"? Consider writing it on your bathroom mirror, leaving a sticky note in your car, setting it as your phone's background, or setting a daily reminder on your phone.

TALKING TO JESUS PART 1

Being a part of God's family has been one of the most profound blessings of my life. I've been richly blessed by the body coming together not only to support me when I needed it but to encourage me as well. Through my church, there's an incredible community of people that I've been able to meet. One of these people is my friend Josh.

Our occasional coffee meetups are where we open up about our lives, share stories, and catch up on everything. Our conversations often revolve around God, the books we're currently engrossed in, and our shared interests.

One day, as we chatted away, I couldn't help but excitedly mention my pilot's license and my deep-rooted passion for aviation. Josh, then shared with me that he worked at Cessna and suggested that we check out a fantastic dining spot in the service center building on their headquarters campus. I was all in! We set a date, and I eagerly looked forward to it!

The day finally arrived, and my excitement levels were through the roof, like a child entering a Build-A-Bear Workshop! The prospect of being at the Cessna headquarters and wandering through that colossal building filled me with unparalleled excitement. As we stepped inside, the words "Cessna Citation" adorned the building's side, signifying the business jets Cessna manufactures. I was giddy on the inside!

The interior was striking—spacious, immaculate, and exuding a corporate elegance. Adorned with sleek artwork of jets, the walls added to the overall charm. I couldn't help but inquire why this place was so impressive, and Josh explained, "This is the customer center, where jet owners come for service."

Right after we entered, there was a security desk in the middle of the lobby, impossible to miss or circumvent. Six individuals were stationed there, diligently checking names and ensuring the building's security.

Approaching the desk, one of the ladies stopped us and asked, "What brings you here?" I pointed to Josh and said, "I'm with him!" Internally, I silently pleaded, "Please don't send me away!"

In response, Josh promptly displayed his company badge to the lady, who then glanced at me once more. I pointed toward Josh again, and she handed me a guest badge that I was instructed to wear. It felt as if I had been granted access to Air Force One or something equally exclusive. We ascended to one the building's higher floors, where we found the restaurant with its enormous windows offering a breathtaking view of the airplanes on the tarmac.

Being in that restaurant, looking out at the airplanes, was an experience I'll never forget. It was genuinely one of the coolest things I've ever had the privilege of doing.

All of this got me thinking about the word "access." If it weren't for Josh's access, I would have never made it up to that restaurant, let alone past the security desk. It made me realize the incredible value of having the right access.

Through Jesus, we gain access to God and Heaven. Jesus is our gateway! Thanks to Him, we have complete and unrestricted access to God, as He has washed away our sins and made us blameless in God's eyes.

DIVINE ACCESS

We have the incredible privilege of connecting with the Almighty Creator, thanks to our faith in Jesus Christ as our Lord and Savior. This extraordinary access is an integral part of our adoption into God's family, a concept beautifully articulated in the book of Romans:

In view of all this, what can we say? If God is for us, who can be against us? Since he did not spare even his own Son but gave him up for us all, won't he also give us everything else? "Therefore, having been justified by faith, we have peace with God through our Lord Jesus Christ, through whom also we have access by faith into this grace in which we stand, and rejoice in hope of the glory of God. (Romans 5:1-2 NIV)

Our right standing with God, which is a result of Jesus's sacrifice on the cross, brings us an inner peace with God, allowing us to draw closer to Him. Before our salvation, we didn't have the privilege of a personal relationship with Him, nor were we considered part of His divine family.

Now, as a person of faith, you belong to Him. He deeply cares about every aspect of your life, and through Jesus, He has granted you the wonderful opportunity to be in communion with Him. Your faith is your key to this remarkable connection. There's a special way to unlock this divine privilege as a member of God's family, and it's through the practice of prayer.

Prayer is a simple yet profound concept; it's essentially having a conversation with Jesus. You may have come across the idea of prayer before, perhaps you already have a routine of talking to God in the morning, during the day, or in the evening. On the other hand, you might be entirely new to the concept of prayer, unsure of what it entails. No matter where you are in your journey of faith, prayer is a powerful tool available to you.

Regardless of the next steps you need to take, it's highly probable that they will come to light through prayer. Prayer is a fundamental aspect of our faith, and the beautiful thing is that there's no secret formula for it, nor is there a need for someone special to do it on our behalf.

While having others pray for us and pray over us can be impactful, prayer is ultimately a deeply personal experience. It's a means for us to communicate with God on a daily basis, allowing us to strengthen our connection with Him. The beauty of prayer lies in its boundless accessibility.

The possibilities are endless, and anyone, anytime, anywhere can pray about anything that weighs on their heart. You are not confined to praying solely in the morning or at night. There are no constraints limiting you to praying only within the walls of a church or during small group gatherings. In fact, there are no rules or prerequisites for prayer.

Prayer is not about adhering to a strict set of rules or performing elaborate rituals. Prayer is not about measuring success or using it to accomplish things. Jesus will reveal to you things that He wants you to chase after through prayer-that can be guaranteed. When He does, He'll help you do those things, but prayer is not primarily about getting things done to get ahead. It's for sure not about getting God to submit to our will either. Prayer is about us submitting to Jesus allowing Him to align our hearts with His. Prayer is way more about connection to Jesus than anything else. Connection to Jesus is vital to sustain life to the fullest. I love Jesus' words about our connection to Him found the book of John. "I am the vine; you are the branches. If you remain in me and I in you, you will bear much fruit; apart from me you can do nothing. (John 15:5 VIV)

Prayer is about your connection to Jesus more than anything else.

Prayer is an opportunity to open our hearts, sharing our thoughts and concerns, and seeking His guidance, love, and grace in our lives. So, no matter where you are on your faith journey, remember that prayer is a powerful and personal way to connect with God, anytime, anywhere.

WHY WE SHOULD USE OUR ACCESS

In the book of 1 Peter, we find these words about prayer: "Humble yourselves, therefore, under God's mighty hand, that he may lift you up in due time. Cast all your anxiety on him because he cares for you." (1 Peter 5:6-7 NIV)

The reason we should use our gift of prayer is because of how Jesus cares. Prayer is an opportunity for me to humble my heart and get beneath God's guidance which is far better than my own understanding. For me, knowing that I have someone capable of carrying not just the burden of my sins but also the weight of life's challenges is incredibly soothing. The as-surance of Jesus's deep care means I'm never truly alone, regardless of what I'm going through.

Whenever I bring something to Jesus in prayer, His response is con-sistently marked by compassion, love, kindness, or correction if He knows I need correcting. His wisdom and guidance always shine through. Sometimes, as I pray about a concern, I'm struck by a sudden insight that I know I could never have thought of on my own.

For me, the most beautiful aspect of prayer is that when I pause to sur-render my worries and fears to Jesus, a profound sense of peace is found. It's a calming reassuring stillness.

That, my friends, is truly invaluable. The fact that we have this incred-ible access to God leaves me in awe, making me wonder how I managed the first eighteen years of my life without prayer.

I'm eager to journey with you into the next chapter where we'll ex-plore the essence of prayer and what it can mean for you. Before we wrap up this chapter on access and the significance of prayer, there's something crucial I want to share with you.

When I found salvation and started my journey with Jesus, I began to pray and share various aspects of my life with Him. However, I stumbled upon something unexpected.

In my conversations with Jesus through prayer, I realized that He doesn't just want fragments of my life, nor does He settle for only half of it; rather, He desires every part of it. He wants to be intimately involved in ev-erything I do, ranging from my career, hobbies, thoughts, actions, friends, purchases, possessions, and even my finances.

Sometimes, I would bring Him my worries, only to find Him saying, "Yes, I understand your concerns, but what about your career? I care about that, too." His level of care astounded me, and I've come to realize that there's absolutely nothing that Jesus isn't willing to be a part of, and there's nothing that frightens Him away. Nothing can deter Him.

What's truly remarkable is that when we grant Him access to our lives in the same way He's given us access to Him, our lives become enriched! Isn't that incredible?

For instance, when I discovered that Jesus desired involvement in my financial matters, I began granting Him access. The more I allowed Him to take control of my finances, the healthier both my heart and bank account became. The same principle applies to my career. When I entrusted Jesus with that aspect of my life, His guidance became crystal clear, and His direction became evident. I have never regretted giving Him more control because every time, He makes my life better than I could have imagined.

Jesus doesn't care about some of your
life, He cares about all your life.

Jesus isn't content with being confined to a Sunday ritual. He longs to be an integral part of every single day of your week. He wants it all! It might sound daunting, but relinquishing control to the One who created the seas, mountains, moon, sun, and stars is profoundly liberating. After all, He truly does have the whole world in His hands.

The book of Colossians offers us a profound perspective:

For you died, and your life is now hidden with Christ in God. When Christ, who is your life, appears, then you also will appear with him in glory. (Colossians 3:3-4 NIV)

Notice, it doesn't say, "Christ, who is a part of your life," or "Christ who claims only Sundays of your week," nor does it even hint at "Christ, who only wants to be a part of your relationships." No, it boldly declares, "Christ WHO IS your life."

Jesus desires not just a fraction of your existence, but the entirety of it. Jesus isn't seeking a part-time role as God in your life; He yearns to be fully immersed in every aspect of your journey, all driven by His immense love for you. That's the extent of His care for you and your experiences in life.

To better visualize this, see the wheel graphic that helps us assess how much control we've surrendered to Him. For most of us, our lives resemble a pie chart where it's evident that many of us have allotted only a small slice of our lives to Christ. Yet, His desire is to encompass it all, to be the central force guiding us in every endeavor, challenge, and joy we encounter.

My Life

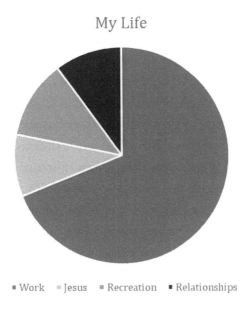

■ Work   ■ Jesus   ■ Recreation   ■ Relationships

We often divide our lives into various compartments, each holding a special place for what matters most to us. Naturally, finances occupy a significant portion of our life, and our career rightfully commands attention. This is the way many of us lead our lives, trying to organize everything neatly, as if faith is a separate entity that needs its own designated space.

Now, I invite you to take a moment to reconsider your entire life. Who has been the driving force behind your decisions? Who has guided you? So far, it has likely been primarily you, perhaps with the occasional input from a family member, mentor, or friend. But your new life in Christ is intended to be different from the one described above. If you've been following Jesus for some time and have never contemplated your life from this perspective, now is the perfect moment to make some adjustments.

Rather than pondering where Jesus fits into your life, let's explore how Jesus envisions it:

Jesus doesn't want to be squeezed into a corner of your life; He desires to be at the center. He wants to shape your choices, guide your steps, and influence every aspect of your existence. Imagine your life as a canvas, and Jesus as the master artist, painting a masterpiece of purpose and fulfillment. When you allow Him to take the lead, your life becomes a beautiful tapestry of faith, love, and purpose. It's not about slotting Him in; it's about surrendering everything to Him.

In this new perspective, you'll find that your career, finances, and every other aspect of your life align with your faith in Christ. Your decisions are no longer solely driven by personal ambitions but are guided by a higher purpose. It's a transformative shift where your relationship with Jesus isn't an isolated segment but the very core of your existence.

So, as you embark on this journey of reimagining your life, remember that it's not about fitting Jesus into your existing framework; it's about allowing Him to create a new and extraordinary masterpiece where He is the focal point. Embrace this new perspective, and you'll discover a life of profound meaning, purpose, and fulfillment in Christ.

Jesus Christ Is My Life - He Is Above It All

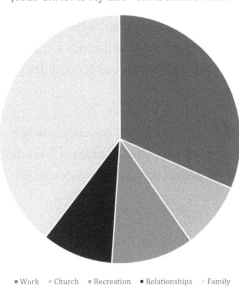

■ Work   ▨ Church   ■ Recreation   ■ Relationships   ▨ Family

He desires the entirety of it. The more you willingly give to Him, the more you'll experience newfound freedom, inner peace, and boundless joy. Keep in mind that Jesus always gives life, never diminishes it.

So, the more of our life we surrender to Jesus in prayer, the more fulfilling our life will become. The more freedom we will find and the more purpose we'll discover.

The more we surrender to Jesus the more we live life to the fullest.

MOMENT OF REFLECTION

- Are there some parts of your life that you have withheld from Jesus? What is keeping you from surrendering control of that area over to Him? You might be wondering, "how can I even take the first step to do this?" It's natural for these questions to seem daunting or intimidating. We'll dive into the practical aspects of handing over control to Jesus, exploring what it entails and how daily prayer plays an integral role in this transformative journey.

- Prayer is a remarkable way to connect with Jesus daily, granting you a profound sense of peace, freedom, and joy that stems from His presence. This chapter emphasizes the significance of inviting Jesus into every aspect of your life, not just a portion of it. What do you think taking time to connect with Jesus daily could look like for you?

- As you reflect on this chapter, consider how it resonates with you. Have you ever contemplated the idea of Jesus desiring your entire life? What challenges do you anticipate encountering on this journey?

- If you've been walking the path of faith with Jesus for some time, take a moment to evaluate whether your life aligns with the concept of the two wheels mentioned earlier. Are there adjustments you believe are necessary?

- Furthermore, think about someone in your life with whom you can share the insights from this chapter. Engaging in meaningful conversations about faith can be transformative.

TALKING TO JESUS PART 2

Since my earliest memories, airplanes have held a special place in my heart. The fascination with flight and all its variations has been an enduring passion of mine. To me, flying represents one of humanity's most remarkable feats, for when you're aboard an airplane, you're defying gravity itself!

In the winter of 2019, following a nudge from Jesus and considerable contemplation and discussions with Allison, I made a life-changing decision: I would embark on the journey to obtain my pilot's license. Jesus wanted to bring this desire out from within me and make a reality.

Assigned to me as an instructor at the flight school was a remarkable individual named Jess, with whom I still maintain contact to this very day. Jess shares my love for flying and faith in God. He guided me in harnessing my faith to overcome the doubts that loomed over my ability to pass the rigorous pilot exams.

During our lessons, there were moments when Jess endeavored to teach me the intricacies of landing an aircraft. There were instances when I executed landings with such force that we would rebound into the sky. But we persevered, continuously honing my skills and learning from the errors and trials.

As I reflect on honing my flying skills, it was really only by practicing, not chasing perfection, that I got better and better. Eventually, I didn't see taking the test as such a big deal anymore because I had spent so many hours practicing what I thought at first would be insurmountable.

I am happy to report to you that in January of 2020 I did in fact finish getting my pilot's license! It's so amazing having this kind of ability to fly whenever I want. It's so cool and I praise Jesus for it! I would not have that license if not for Him. Like I said, it was only by practice that I got better even when it was awkward, and I didn't understand what Jess was trying to teach me.

My experience of getting my license and learning to pray were very similar experiences for me. Both were awkward at first. Both were hard at first. I didn't know or understand what to do at first.

I grappled with uncertainties about what to pray for, how to converse with God, and whether I might inadvertently upset Him with my words or actions. The questions surrounding prayer were genuine, and I suspect many of you can relate.

I aim to offer insights into these questions and provide you with a prayer approach you can start using right away. It's crucial to understand that there's no way to fail at prayer. It's not a test or a task to complete like we said in the last chapter. It's not about measurables and goals. Instead, prayer is all about nurturing a meaningful connection.

WHAT PRAYER IS NOT

Prayer isn't some magical formula to grant all our wishes. God isn't a genie we summon to fulfill our wishes, nor a bank ready to grant our every whim. He's not there to make us rich either. We should appreciate that He's not here to make us billionaires. In fact, it might even offend Him to think that prayer's sole purpose is to acquire wealth and material gains. While there might be instances where God blesses us in such ways, that's not the purpose of prayer. As humans, we need much more than just to be served.

It's not a performance either. You won't earn extra points with your Heavenly Father based on the eloquence of your prayers because He already loves you more than you can fathom. As a child of God, your prayers won't change your standing with Him.

> Praying is not about seeking approval; we
> pray from a position of approval.

Think about what these verses highlight about approaching God with confidence:

Do your best to present yourself to God as one approved, a worker who does not need to be ashamed and who correctly handles the word of truth. (2 Timothy 2:15 NIV)

Let us then approach God's throne of grace with confidence, so that we may receive mercy and find grace to help us in our time of need. (Hebrews 4:16 NIV)

When we pray to God, we do so with confidence because of our standing. We're not approaching Him as beggars fearing harm or rejection. Instead, we go to Him because He genuinely loves and cares for us.

IS THERE A WRONG WAY TO PRAY?

I'm from the charming small town of Lavonia, nestled in the heart of North Georgia. I love my hometown and I loved growing up in Franklin County. Georgia is situated in the southeastern part of the United States which brings with it a unique trait: a distinct accent.

Some accents are more pronounced than others, but in the South, we all have one, no matter how thick or subtle it may be. I remember when I first tried to navigate prayer. I found myself uttering heartfelt words in my southern drawl, something like, "Jesus, I wanna talk with ya, I need ya. Come on down now and help me live life with ya." If you've experienced the South, you'll know exactly what I mean!

Yet, I couldn't help but wonder, does Jesus comprehend my words? Can He even understand southern slang? Then I pondered further—can

He understand Spanish? What about Thai? Or Yankee talk from New York? My curiosity led me to dig deeper, and I discovered that one of God's defining attributes is His omniscience or His ability to know everything like we mentioned earlier in this book. There is nothing beyond God's knowledge, for it contradicts His very nature.

Friends, there's good news! Since there's nothing God doesn't know He understands us. He speaks Thai, He speaks southern, He speaks northern, and He understands Spanish. In prayer, there is no wrong way to speak because prayer revolves around being genuine to yourself and God, and that's precisely who Jesus desires you to be. He wants the genuine you. He genuinely desires a true relationship with you! When I contemplate prayer and whether there are erroneous methods, I can only think of one example that is most definitely a wrong way to pray. Jesus clearly warns against a prayer that is intended solely to impress God or others.

Jesus imparts this wisdom regarding such prayers:

And when you pray, do not be like the hypocrites, for they love to pray standing in the synagogues and on the street corners to be seen by others. Truly I tell you, they have received their reward in full. But when you pray, go into your room, close the door and pray to your Father, who is unseen. Then your Father, who sees what is done in secret, will reward you. (Matthew 6:5-6, NIV)

I admire how Jesus emphasizes that prayer is a vehicle for building a personal relationship with God, not a tool for impressing others. It is indeed beneficial to pray within a group because there is tremendous power when a collective voice rises to God. However, it boils down to the motive within your heart. Are you praying before others due to selfish motives, or are you joining them in prayer because all of you are earnestly seeking God's guidance and intervention?

Think of prayer not as a mere duty but as a lifeline. As new creations in Christ, prayer should be our initial response to any situation in life. There's no need to fear or hesitate in bringing everything to Jesus. He already knows what's happening, and He eagerly desires to be involved in every aspect of our lives. Embrace prayer as the cornerstone of your connection with Him.

HOW TO HAVE A QUIET TIME

While there's no secret formula for prayer, I want to give you a starting point—a simple framework, if you will. By no means am I saying that this is the right way or the only way.

When I embarked on my journey of writing devotionals, my mentor didn't just toss me a computer with a blank screen and wish me luck. She took the time to explain the significance of devotionals, guiding me step by step through the process. She provided me with a foundation to work from, a solid starting point as she guided me through writing training.

Her mentorship allowed me to navigate what it meant to create a devotional. I would've been lost with no starting point if not for her leadership that I'm so grateful for.

That's precisely what I'd like to offer you, a simple starting point. As time goes on, add your own personal touch to your prayer time, like seasoning your favorite dish with your unique sauce. Make it yours and find what personally stirs your heart and affection for Jesus. Remember, there's no magic formula or one right way to pray.

Personally, I call my prayer time my "quiet time." You don't have to use the same term, but since 2013, it's what I've called it. It's my special time in the early morning when everything is calm, and I'm the only one awake. During this time, I try to focus on Jesus without any distractions. Your quiet time, just like mine, is a dedicated moment to connect with God. It can be as brief as ten minutes, or it can stretch to a full hour, or even longer. This is an uninterrupted part of your day when you set aside everything else and simply be with your Creator. Something I heard a pastor say years ago has stuck with me, "ten minutes a day with Jesus will change the rest of your days."

It's a time to commune with Jesus, allowing Him to speak to your heart, mind, and soul. The more you embrace these quiet moments, the stronger your yearning for more of Jesus becomes—there's truly nothing quite like it.

In the Old Testament of the Bible, we find the story of Moses, who led the nation of Israel to freedom. Moses had his own quiet times with God, and I'm fascinated by how the book of Exodus describes them:

The Lord would speak to Moses face to face, as one speaks to a friend. (Exodus 33:11 NIV)

I love that verse so much. It is such a sweet explanation of what time with the Lord is like. That verse displays God's heart so well.

As you spend more time in the presence of God, you'll likely find yourself echoing the sentiment of this verse from Psalms: "As the deer pants for streams of water, so my soul pants for you, my God. My soul thirsts for God, for the living God. When can I go and meet with God?" (Psalm 42:1-2 NIV).

This question beautifully illustrates that our quiet time is the pinnacle of living life to the fullest as a new creation. When can I go and meet with God?

Not only do we experience fulfillment in Jesus's presence, but He also provides clarity for life's decisions. He helps you understand the path to follow and guides you on your journey.

The book of Psalms reassures us: "You make known to me the path of life; you will fill me with joy in your presence, with eternal pleasures at your right hand" (Psalm 16:11 NIV).

I see my quiet time through the lens of these scriptures. It's an opportunity to meet with God, to be heard, listened to, and cared for. It's a time to be guided through life's twists and turns because God's wisdom surpasses my own.

Here's a glimpse into the framework I try and use. Sometimes I deviate but for the most part this is where I try and live. You certainly don't have to use this because like I've said, it's not "the perfect way" it's just my way that I love that helps me connect with Jesus. Feel free to take from it what you wish or use all of it.

Whether you're just starting your journey with Jesus, or you've been walking with Him for decades, there's something valuable for everyone in the outline below. Let's dive in:

1. Thankfulness

Start each day with gratitude. It's incredible how being thankful can uplift your heart and mind. Personally, I make it a daily practice to find something to be grateful for. It can be the same thing several days in a row or something new every day. I express gratitude for my job, for Allison, my parents, my home, the money in my bank account, my friends, my car, or my clothes.

A memorable lesson I learned from a teacher in ministry school was about thanking God for even the simplest things, like our shoes. It struck me because it highlighted that we can express gratitude for anything, not just the big stuff.

Gratitude doesn't always have to revolve around significant blessings like a new home or job. It can extend to everyday things like the food in our fridge, the ability to access the pharmacy for necessary medicine, or any other aspect of our lives. Scripture underscores the importance of approaching God with gratitude:

Enter his gates with thanksgiving and his courts with praise; give thanks to him and praise his name. For the Lord is good and his love endures forever; his faithfulness continues through all generations. (Psalm 100:4-5 NIV)

Coming to God with a heart full of gratitude sets the stage for us to focus on what God might reveal to us each day. It not only improves our attitude but also directs our attention toward the good in our lives.

2. Forgiveness

I recognize that I am far from perfect, and I'll never attain perfection. This is why I constantly yearn for forgiveness. I may not like to admit it, but I commit sins every single day. There's a particular verse that resonates with me regarding the need for daily forgiveness:

> In the book of James 4:17 (NIV), it is written: "If anyone, then, knows the good they ought to do and doesn't do it, it is sin for them."

I don't know about you, but I frequently fall short of the standards set in this verse. You can replace "the good" with "the right thing," as some translations suggest. You might relate to falling short as well. When you find yourself in need of forgiveness, turn to God. If you struggle with being kind to people during the day, ask God to help you overcome this and seek His forgiveness for mistreating others. If you battle with a particular temptation, ask God for assistance in that area and seek His forgiveness for your wrongdoing.

You might wonder, "Didn't I receive forgiveness when I accepted Jesus?" The answer is yes. When you seek forgiveness in your quiet time, it's not because you're unsaved or have lost your salvation; such a loss is impossible. You're simply acknowledging the truth that none of us can live a perfect life and asking Jesus for His help.

3. Listen

It's crucial to emphasize that our moments of quiet reflection should revolve around listening and waiting for God's guidance. Some mornings, as I sit down for my quiet time, I find myself simply listening, allowing the presence of God to fill me. I want to assure you that He will indeed lead and guide you down the right path. Sometimes, He might impress a specific scripture upon your heart, urging you to search for it. Other times, He may plant a thought in your mind that opens your eyes to something profound.

When I receive guidance during my quiet time, I follow it up with a prayer. If it's a call to take a step, I pray for confidence. If it's a request to wait a little longer, I pray for patience. Whatever direction Jesus is leading you toward as you listen, offer it back to Him in prayer.

4. Prayer list

Moving on to the next step in my prayer routine: the prayer list. Here, I dedicate time to pray for various things. This can include people you are praying for. It could be someone you want to see come to know Jesus. Someone you know that needs Jesus to do something in their life or concerns about global events. Making others a part of your prayer list is vital. I also pray for the good and pure desires God has placed in my heart. One of the most rewarding practices I've adopted is what I call my "pray and wait" list.

I can't recall who first taught me this, but it's been a game changer. I jot down on a whiteboard those desires I believe are genuine and in alignment with God's will. Each day, I pray over these items. When God answers one of these prayers, I mark it. This way, I can look back and see how God has moved in my life.

I do understand it's important for you to have examples of what goes on a prayer list so in the next chapter we are going to talk more about what it looks like to have faith for God to do something. I'll show you a couple things on my prayer list that I have faith for.

In the following chapters, we'll dive into how to pray for the things you believe in, using your own prayer list.

5. Read Scripture or a Devotional and Then Pray It

One of my favorite books in the Bible is Psalms. During my quiet time, I often turn to Psalms or other books I wish to explore.

Here are a couple of verses from Psalms that I'd like to share with you:

Who may ascend the mountain of the Lord? Who may stand in His holy place? The one who has clean hands and a pure heart, who does not trust in an idol or swear by a false god. (Psalm 24:3 NIV)

When I read this scripture, I turn it into a prayer. I might pray, "Jesus, help me live with clean hands and a pure heart. Enable me to have more of you in my life. I want to honor you in my thoughts and actions. Help me, Jesus, to live this way."

Unless the Lord builds the house, the builders labor in vain. (Psalm 127:1 NIV)

For this scripture, my prayer might sound like, "Jesus, come and help me build my life with you as the foundation. Help me desire more of you and less of me." If you're just starting to read the Bible, consider diving into the Psalms and see what resonates with you. Additionally, I recommend the book of John in the New Testament. John, one of Jesus's disciples, offers a firsthand account of Jesus's life. Perhaps start by reading one chapter a day during your quiet time.

Another practice I often engage in is reading a short devotional or watching a video that unpacks a piece of scripture. There are countless resources available and there's no single right way to do this. However, I firmly believe that if you open God's word and start reading, He will meet you on those pages, offering you valuable insights and clarity. Something that happened to me recently that involved my Bible was this:

While traveling through Greenville Spartanburg International Airport in Greenville, South Carolina, I was stopped by a TSA agent at the security checkpoint. He noticed something unusual in my bag and asked me to show it to him.

To his surprise, it was my Bible. He took it from me, held it in his hands, and with a smile on his face, said, "It warms my heart to see someone with a Bible. Not many people I know read the Bible anymore, son. Great job, and never, ever give up on your faith."

6. Life-Giving Words

About two years ago, I started crafting my own set of life-giving words. These affirmations serve as a daily reminder to align myself with God's perspective before I embark on my day. I encourage you to create your own set of truths to hold onto. I recite these words at the end of my quiet time each day, and if I ever find myself in a situation where confidence wavers, I try and silently repeat them in my mind. Here they are:

> I am a loved child of God. I am a loving husband. I am a leader who empowers others to lead. I am creative and innovative. God's radiant love shines through me.

These words have been instrumental in my life, providing a consistent source of truth that I can memorize and affirm every single day. Sometimes, we all need a reminder of who we truly are. Think about creating your own life-giving words and place them where you can easily access them—in your phone, on a mirror, or in your car.

TOUCH OF HEAVEN

Going to Jesus daily in prayer is an opportunity for our hearts to be filled. Our part in this opportunity is to simply turn our hearts to Jesus. There's an abundance of peace, love and joy to be found in this time with Jesus. There's a song I love called "Touch Of Heaven" and some of the lyrics go like this,

"How I live for the moments where I'm still in your presence, all noise dies down, Lord speak to me now. You have all my attention; I will linger and listen. I can't miss a thing. Lord I know my heart wants more of you, my heart wants something new so I surrender all. All I want, is to live within your love, be undone by who you are, my desire is to know you deeper, Lord, I will open up again, throw my fears into the wind, I am desperate for a touch of heaven."

The lyrics of this song remind me so much of how desperate I am for Jesus. I need Him more than anything. I need His presence, His love, His care, His provision, His wisdom and peace. I am dependent on Jesus for everything. He is the source of my supply. He fills my bucket with living water just He filled Emma's heart that day at the well.

We are the ones who are dependent on Jesus and who He is. A verse in the book of Romans says it like this: So then, everything depends, not on what we humans want or do, but only on God's mercy. (Romans 9:16 GNT)

I want to challenge you here, are you dependent on Jesus to be your source? If not, what is the well that you are running to? Our efforts are good but nothing like Jesus and what He has for us. Following Jesus is not about what we can do for Him, but rather what He has already done for us. Allow Him to be your source and practice dependence every single day. Jesus doesn't need our eloquent words or sometimes any words at all. He wants our hearts and for us to depend on Him as our source because everything in this world will always fall short of the glory of God.

My part is turning my heart to Jesus.

Use the steps mentioned above to kickstart your journey of having a quiet time with God. Keep in mind that, over time, you'll develop your own routines and habits for this special time. There isn't a one-size-fits-all approach to quiet times; they're not about the method but rather about these three fundamental aspects:

1. Relationship: Deepening your connection with God.
2. Remaining Connected Scripture: Staying rooted in God's word.
3. Becoming More Like Jesus: Experiencing transformation and growth in your faith journey.

It's far less about the method as it is your connection to Jesus. Jesus wants to hear from you. Talk to Him and share your concerns. Share your heart and thoughts with Him. He longs to spend time with you every single day.

MOMENT OF REFLECTION

- Choose a comfortable place: Find a spot where you feel safe and at ease. For me, it's our downstairs office, but it could be your bedroom, kitchen table, your living room couch or on your drive to work in the mornings.

- Establish a consistent time: Consistency is key to a successful quiet time routine. Determine a specific time that works for you. If it's in the evening, tell yourself, "Every night at seven p.m. is my quiet time," or if it's in the morning, say, "Every morning at six a.m. is my quiet time."

- Start journaling: Consider keeping a journal. It's a valuable practice. Writing down your thoughts and experiences during your quiet time can be incredibly enlightening. I still have my journal from when I began my journey with Jesus in 2013, and it's amazing to revisit my thoughts about God from back then. It also helps you track and appreciate how God has been working in your life.

- Get a Bible either in digital or physical form: The YouVersion Bible app is a great digital Bible. My favorite is a physical Bible because I love to highlight and make notes on the pages. Do what works for you and what stirs your hunger for God's word. However you get a Bible, remember, your Bible is yours and it's how Jesus wants to reveal Himself to you. Highlight that thing up and make notes in it.

- Lastly, what well do you run to as your source? Practice daily dependence on Jesus to be the source of your supply. His well never runs dry.

FAITH FOR _____.

Growing up in Georgia, I had two beloved college football teams: the University of Georgia Bulldogs and the University of Clemson Tigers. My hometown was within a thirty-minute drive to both schools. In the South, college football is a religion. In my hometown, you could go to the grocery store on game day and a random person would say to you, "You see Georgia plays today, didn't you? You think they have a chance?"

This was during the years 2002-2008, when I was in elementary and middle school. I have to admit, both teams were pretty average during that time, nothing that would make you jump for joy.

Every Saturday in the fall, as Georgia prepared to play, I'd turn to my family or friends and ask, "Do you think Georgia and Clemson have a chance today?" The response was always a sobering, "Don't get your hopes up, boy." That response summed it up perfectly because both these teams were like an emotional rollercoaster. It was akin to scratching off a lottery ticket and winning nothing for the fifth time in a row. Every Saturday, you'd hope for the best, only to be left disappointed.

However, things took a turn for the better when Clemson brought in a fantastic coach named Dabo Swinney. From then 'til now, that program has undergone a dramatic transformation. In the year 2014, Clemson started to gain national prominence that had eluded Clemson since the 1980s.

My favorite of these two teams, Clemson, has consistently won their league championship almost every year, with multiple national championships to their name, firmly establishing themselves as an elite team.

Georgia also found their way in recent years. They brought in Kirby Smart, who used to be an assistant coach for the Alabama Crimson Tide (roll tears!), and he completely turned the program around. Georgia celebrated their first national championship win since the 1980s in 2022.

While I have an undying passion for college football and watching these two teams play every Saturday (Go Tigers!), I want to reflect on something I was repeatedly told when I was growing up, especially on Saturdays before watching the games:

"Don't get your hopes up, boy."

Have you ever heard that advice? Has someone cautioned you not to get your hopes up because, well, "what if it doesn't happen?" Perhaps you've been hearing this for so long that you've decided it's just not worth the heartache to get your hopes up about anything anymore.

Maybe there have been times when you had high hopes for someone to come through for you, only to be let down repeatedly. As a result, you've resigned yourself to thinking, "It's not even worth getting excited about anymore because I know how this will end." Or perhaps you've contemplated making significant changes in your life.

But every time you took a step toward your goal, disappointment seemed to follow. So, you've thrown in the towel.

NOT YOURSELF, BUT JESUS

When we embrace Jesus as our Lord and Savior, our lives undergo a profound transformation. We shift from placing our faith solely in ourselves to placing it in Him. Relying solely on our own abilities and understanding can only take us so far, for we are but fallible humans.

When we make ourselves the sole source of hope, we find ourselves coming up short because we were never created to be our own god. Placing your hope in yourself leads to feeling hopeless. In such moments, phrases like "don't ever get your hopes up" and "on the other side of hope is disappointment" come into play. While these statements hold some truth in certain circumstances, they do not encompass the entirety of our existence.

Consider a scenario where you stand beside an electric fence, hoping it won't shock you when you touch it. In this case, it's safe to say that disappointment and perhaps a significant amount of pain await you on the other side of that hope. Or imagine you have a craving for a delicious creamy milkshake from your local McDonald's. You eagerly arrive at the restaurant, anticipating that sweet treat, only to be told the disheartening news: the ice cream machine is broken! This is another instance where disappointment indeed lurks on the other side of hope. However, these examples of disappointment differ significantly from the hope we can find in Jesus. He surpasses the delight of a milkshake or avoiding an electric shock.

Jesus encourages us to raise our hopes high, to become excited about our future, and to eagerly anticipate His work in our lives. Jesus has the power to lead us to places we never envisioned ourselves going and to reveal talents and qualities within us that we never knew existed. We anchor our hope in the One who conquered the grave, defeated death, and faithfully promises to be with us always.

BELIEVE FOR IT

King Saul was the first king of Israel and while he was king his notorious enemy was the Philistines. The Israelites and the Philistines had been fighting and the Philistines had taken up camp in Israel. One day Saul was camping out under a pomegranate tree contemplating what move to make next with about six hundred of his soldiers and his son named Jonathan.

Jonathan did not want to wait any longer. He had a wild idea that would either stretch his trust in God or get him killed. His wild idea was to sneak away from his father's camp to go to where the Philistines were without the army to support him. Jonathan recruits his young armor bearer who was responsible for carrying weapons to go with him to the Philistines. Scripture says it like this:

> One day Jonathan, son of Saul, said to his young armor-bearer, "Come, let's go over to the Philistine outpost on the other side." But he did not tell his father. (1 Samuel 14:1 NIV)

Jonathan was not interested in waiting for his father, Saul, to make up his mind. Jonathan had a wild faith about him. He didn't wait for his father's approval or ask him for his opinion. He wasn't interested in playing it safe. He was living out his trust in God. Scripture says this is what Jonathan said when he and his armor bearer were approaching the Philistines:

> Jonathan said to his young armor-bearer, "Come let's go over to those uncircumcised men. Perhaps the Lord will act on our behalf. Nothing can hinder the Lord from saving, whether by many or by few." (1 Samuel 14:6 NIV)

I love how Jonathan declares his trust in the Lord by saying "perhaps the Lord will act on our behalf," and then he proceeds to move on toward them! It would have been so easy for him to set sight on the Philistines and see he was outnumbered. Or even to sit under the pomegranate tree with his father waiting, perplexed about what to do.

Not Jonathan-he took hold of his faith and applied it trusting that God would come through for him. As Jonathan and his armor bearer went on toward the Philistines, scripture says that the Lord shook the ground and sent a panic on the Philistines. Jonathan ended up killing twenty Philistines and won the battle all because of his trust in God. He dared to believe God for it.

Jonathan believed big. He exercised bold faith. He didn't say "I shouldn't be getting my hopes up," or "This could go sideways really fast." Better yet, he didn't even start counting the resources he had, saying "We've got two shields, three spears, and a sackcloth. They have way more weapons than us."

Jonathan had faith for God to come through for him. Just like this, Jesus wants us to move off faith. He wants to trust Him and believe boldly. Jesus wants to stir up the faith within you not contain it. You have a lion deep down on the inside and Jesus is calling it to come out. I believe God is waiting to take some of us to new levels, but it's going to require much larger faith then what we currently have.

> Jesus wants to stir up the desires He's
> placed within your heart.

What desires do you have on the inside of you that you want to see God do? What is it that you sense God stirring your faith for? What is on the inside of you that's trying to come out, but your fear won't let it?

There is a beautiful song that I love when pondering the hidden desires God has placed deep down inside of me. Things that I really want to see God do someday that will only bring Him more honor and glory. The song is called "Believe for it" by CeCe Winans and some of the lyrics go like this:

"They say these mountains can't be moved, they say these chains will never break, but they don't know you like we do, there is power in your name, we've heard that there's no way through, we've heard the tide will never change, they haven't seen what you can do, there is power in your name, so much power in your name."

Jesus wants to bring those out of you. He wants to see you place your faith in Him over trust in yourself. The world will tell you to count your resources, look at where you are, look at your family history, or look at where you are currently employed. It's not possible. You don't have what it takes. It doesn't add up.

The best way to gain confidence and clarity for these things is to go to Jesus in prayer about them. Take it to Him and allow Him to lead you. As you get confirmation, keep praying for it to come to pass. Don't give up on whatever it is. The Bible calls this shameless persistence.

SHAMELESS PERSISTENCE

Jesus had a close-knit group of twelve disciples, individuals who were unwaveringly loyal and followed Him wherever He went. These disciples were not mere bystanders; they bore witness to the remarkable events documented in the scriptures.

What's even more fascinating is that four of them are recognized authors of books within the Bible. Matthew, Mark, Luke, and John, all devout followers of Jesus, penned their firsthand accounts of His life. Exploring each of their writings provides a unique window into their distinct perspectives.

Among the disciples, Luke, who was a doctor by profession, stands out for his attention to detail. It's not surprising, considering physicians often possess a distinctive way of thinking. In his writings, Luke shares valuable insights into how Jesus instructed His followers on the subject of prayer. Luke recounts Jesus's teachings on prayer with a compelling story:

> Then, teaching them more about prayer, he used this story: "Suppose you went to a friend's house at midnight, wanting to borrow three loaves of bread. You say to him, 'A friend of mine has just arrived for a visit, and I have nothing for him to eat.' And suppose he calls out from his bedroom, 'Don't bother me. The door is locked for the night, and my family and I are all in bed. I can't help you.' But I tell you this—though he won't do it for friendship's sake, if you keep knocking long enough, he will get up and give you whatever you need because of your shameless persistence." (Luke 11:5-8 NLT)

In this tale, the man inside the house initially appears reluctant to assist his friend—a situation that anyone might find understandable given the late hour. Yet, according to Jesus, the key takeaway is the persistence exhibited by the friend seeking help. He kept knocking persistently, even if it meant potentially annoying the person inside. Ultimately, his unwavering persistence paid off, and he received what he sought.

This narrative evokes memories of a child relentlessly asking their parent, "When are we going to Disney World?" Year after year, the child's persistence never wanes, no matter how many times the parent assures them, "We'll go in the future." In the end, the parent concedes and fulfills the child's dream. It's almost as if this story grants permission to be a bit of a pest at times.

However, there's a deeper truth to this principle. Jesus further elaborates:

> I tell you, keep on asking, and you will receive what you ask for. Keep on seeking, and you will find. Keep on knocking, and the door will be opened to you. For everyone who asks, receives. Everyone who seeks, finds. And to everyone who knocks, the door will be opened. "You fathers—if your children ask for a fish, do you give them a snake instead? Or if they ask for an egg, do you give them a scorpion? Of course not! (Luke 11:9-12 NLT).

Jesus emphasizes the concept of shameless persistence and how it directly applies to our prayers. There's something profound about making this story practical in our own faith journey. Jesus encourages us not only to ask repeatedly but also gives us permission to do so.

Let me clarify one thing: this isn't about the prosperity gospel, far from it. Jesus isn't suggesting that if we keep begging for a million it will happen. He isn't saying that if we beg for expensive, luxurious cars that He will give it to us. And He isn't saying that if we keep begging for our name for fame that He will give it to us. Those are selfish desires. His sacrifice on the cross was not for our selfish desires. We need so much more than just to be served. We need Jesus's transformation in our hearts. We need His grace. We need His love and guidance.

As we employ shameless persistence, we must do so with pure intentions, seeking God's will and honoring Him. Remember, Jesus is not a genie in a bottle, existing solely to fulfill our desires.

The catalyst for significant movements in our lives, according to Jesus, is our faith. When Jesus sees unwavering faith in one of His children, it captures His attention.

So, what do you have faith for? What is it that you need from Him?

I want to share some of my stories in life with you that will shed light on what it means to have faith for Jesus to move and also how to gauge what to have shameless persistent prayer for.

SOME OF MY FAITH FOR ⎯⎯⎯⎯⎯⎯⎯⎯ STORIES

NewSpring College:

In September 2013, when I asked Jesus into my heart, I found myself without any clear career prospects. I was adrift, unsure of my life's purpose. However, I soon realized that I needed to shift my perspective from what I wanted to do to what Jesus wants me to do.

As a new believer, I began to understand that Jesus cared not only about me but also about my career path, as reflected in the concept of life wheels. I started praying over and over about what Jesus might have in store for my career choice, placing my faith in Him to guide me.

One day, while I was praying about this, something incredible happened. Jesus answered me, saying, "You will go into ministry." I knew that Jesus doesn't impress this on everyone who follows Him, as Jesus has diverse missions for different people. Some are called to be lawyers defending the defenseless, doctors healing the sick, farmers feeding populations, or founders of nonprofits focused on health, education, or combating slavery. Others are called to be funeral directors, caregivers, teachers, or even exceptional retail workers.

Once Jesus impressed this in my heart, I made it a daily practice to pray about it using shameless persistence. Without fail, every day, I would pray, "Jesus, you told me to go into ministry. Show me how to do this." That was my shameless persistence prayer.

At that time, I had been attending NewSpring for only five months, from May to September of 2013. I was growing my trust in Jesus and anticipating direction from Him. From October to December, I continued my prayers, and then something remarkable occurred in December of 2013.

I stumbled upon a Facebook post by Brad who is one of the lead pastors. His post declared, "Hey you, NewSpring College is official for the fall of 2014! Apply now."

I can't adequately describe the impact of that moment; it hit me like a ton of bricks. I couldn't hold back tears as they flowed from my eyes. In the midst of my emotions, Jesus whispered in my heart, "This is how I'm going to prepare you." I was left utterly speechless.

When the time came to apply, I took the necessary steps, and to my amazement, I was accepted! Before I knew it, I was enrolled in classes, receiving guidance and instruction from some of the most influential leaders in the modern church today.

Meeting Allison:

I had just graduated from NewSpring College, I had been using the same principle of shameless persistence. Asking Jesus "You led me here to the point, I'm trusting you to show me what's next." I prayed that repeatedly.

One sunny day in Anderson, South Carolina as I checked the mailbox at the house I shared with two friends, my phone rang. The number displayed was unfamiliar, but it showed Minneapolis, Minnesota as the caller's location. Curiosity piqued; I answered the call. A voice on the other end introduced himself and mentioned that he worked with Youthworks, a nonprofit mission trip organization. He inquired if I would consider joining them for the upcoming summer.

Initially, my immediate response was, "No, thank you." I had worked for Youthworks during a previous summer, only to be let go. Who, in their right mind, would willingly return to a company that had once terminated their employment? It didn't seem like a good idea at all, which made no such an answer to tell this guy. But the man persisted, offering me the Christian advice, "You should pray about it."

So, I began to pray and seek guidance from Jesus. Again, in shameless persistence "Jesus, you led me here, I'm trusting you to show me what's next." It became clear to me through praying this that Jesus was telling me—"This job is meant for you." With this conviction, I called the man back a couple of days later and admitted, "You were right." I decided to accept the job offer, despite my initial hesitations.

That summer turned out to be a pivotal one for me. Not only did it provide me with invaluable ministry experience where I had the privilege of preaching to hundreds of teenagers, but it also brought someone special into my life. As I arrived at my assigned site, I met a person who would become a significant blessing—Allison. She greeted me with a friendly, "Hi, my name is Allison, how about you?"

Looking back, I can now clearly see why Jesus had led me to that job and how He had orchestrated our meeting. Allison is undoubtedly the greatest blessing that Jesus has ever bestowed upon me.

Alaska:

I had received the job opportunity at Youthworks where I had met Allison. Upon completion of that job, which ended in August of 2016, I was again asking Jesus "You led me here, I'm trusting you to show me what's next."

While attending NewSpring College, Jesus was stirring my heart for Alaska. I didn't understand at the time so I didn't really give it too much thought, but the desire never went away. I had even started discussing this growing desire with mentors at school. It was all uncharted territory for me, but I was committed to following the path that Jesus had set in my heart. Even after Youthworks was over, I had this desire still in my heart and it grew ever so strongly.

One day, I retreated to my closet, closed the door, and dropped to my knees. I prayed, "Jesus, why is this desire growing in my heart and what should I do about Alaska? Then, as clear as when He instructed me to attend NewSpring College, He simply said, "Go." That's it! Just "go!"

Sometimes Jesus omits the details, encouraging us to exercise the faith He's trying to build within us. This is where I learned that Jesus often operates this way!

I did what I had been doing, started to pray with shameless persistence with unwavering determination, "Jesus, if you want me to do this, show me the way. I don't know how to proceed."

Remarkably, someone I had known for years from NewSpring College randomly texted me; he mentioned that he had a friend who had recently moved to Anchorage, Alaska and had also attended NewSpring. You can't make this stuff up, guys!

I quickly got in touch with this guy who lived in Alaska, his name is Ford, and shared my sense of Jesus's leading. Without hesitation, Ford extended an invitation for me to stay with him in Alaska. So, I purchased an airline ticket and embarked on this unexpected journey. It was incredible—Ford, from the very same church I was attending school at, happened to reside in Alaska! I couldn't help but be amazed at how God was orchestrating all of this.

Ford provided me with a safe place to stay as I explored Alaska and sought out my purpose there. Once again, not only had God ignited a deep desire within me, but He had also paved the way for it to become a reality. He had blessed me and connected me with Ford. It's a testament to how, when the time is right and our hearts are aligned, God continues to show up and never lets us down.

Towel Story:

When I was living in Alaska, I didn't have much to my name, and I found myself in need of a towel. I know, it might sound crazy, and you might be thinking, "go to the store!"

I did what I had been doing in the past. I turned to Jesus in prayer because I wanted to trust Him with a need I had. I prayed with persistence, "Jesus, I need a towel and I trust you to help me." A couple of days later, something incredible happened. A random package showed up at my doorstep in Alaska, and it was sent all the way from Anderson, South Carolina. With excitement, I opened the box, and guess what I found inside? A towel! But that's not all; there were other items in the box that I needed too. The note inside simply said, "God told me to send you this stuff, so here you go."

$375 Plumber Story:

I recall a time when Allison and I had just moved into our new house, and things seemed to be piling up. It's a common occurrence when you get something new; something always needs attention. One day, we faced a plumbing issue, the pipes needed to be snaked from the outside. Essentially, the pipes needed cleaning because it had been neglected for a while. I was nervous because I had never dealt with such expenses before.

When the plumber came and completed the job, he handed us the bill, and it read $375, almost to the penny. I started wondering how we would manage to pay for it, and I couldn't help but worry about what else might go wrong with our new home. $375 was a substantial amount, especially for new homeowners.

I texted Allison, who was at school teaching her students math, and told her about the plumber's bill. She responded, "Bryant, I just received a random check today. How much was the plumber?" I replied, "It was $375, honey." Believe it or not, Allison texted back, "Bryant, this check is made out for $375, almost to the penny!"

I am constantly amazed by what Jesus does in my life. Some might call it luck, but I choose to focus on the fact that Jesus cares and He provides for His kids. What are the odds of receiving a random check for the exact same amount on the very same day? Jesus is good, and He knows our needs even before we do.

I want to ask you again, what do you have faith for? Some folks out there claim that God isn't interested in blessing us or doing something extraordinary in our lives. While it's true that life involves honoring God, I've witnessed God's hand at work in my life in countless ways. So, don't fall into the trap of thinking, "God won't work powerfully in my life."

I've seen Him come through for me when there seemed to be no possible way. He's been a nurturing Father to me.

So, what's your faith focused on?

I'm telling you, raise your expectations! Get excited and prepare yourself. Jesus intends to do something remarkable in your life. He didn't save you just so you could go to heaven for eternity and that's the end of the story. Jesus desires to make a profound impact in your life at this very moment. He has incredible plans for you, things you can't fathom.

Here are some scriptures that reveal how Jesus intends to work in our lives:

Now to him who is able to do immeasurably more than all we can ask or imagine, according to his power that is at work within us. (Ephesians 3:20, NIV)

What no eye has seen and no ear has heard, the things God has prepared for those who love him. (1 Corinthians 2:10, NIV)

So, what are you believing for? What do have faith for? What's in your heart? God has the final say for what's hidden within your heart, not anyone else, and not your circumstances.

Are you believing for guidance in your career? Are you feeling stuck, unsure about choices related to a relationship, job, purchase, health, or something else? Are you believing for generational chains to break? Perhaps you need a friend or mentor to support and guide you. Maybe you're yearning for a family member or friend to discover Jesus. Is it a connection you're seeking in your life? Or do you long for the weight of shame to be lifted from your heart and soul? Could it be that you need a financial breakthrough?

What are the dreams in your heart that scare you, they are so big? Some of you have a desire to own a hospital. Some a desire to have a family. A desire to have your own company. I dare you to believe big and trust Jesus. Release those dreams and desires to Jesus and allow Him to stretch your faith. This book was one of my deep desires for years. I've had the faith for it, it was just not the right time before and Jesus knew that. He brought this out of me at the right time.

MOMENT OF REFLECTION:

Whatever it is that you need and believe Jesus can do, as long as it comes from a place of purity, I believe Jesus wants to act on it. I believe He wants to take action. Psalm 37:5 assures us of this:

> Commit your ways to the Lord, trust in Him, and He will act. (Psalm 37:5, NIV)

Notice, it doesn't say He might, it says He will! I'm confident in this verse because I've personally experienced God's intervention in my life.

Before we moved into our new place, Allison started collecting a massive pile of cardboard boxes. I asked her, "Sweetie, why are you gathering all these boxes? It's not moving time yet." She replied, "Bryant, I'm getting ready to move. I believe it's almost here." Now that's some serious faith! Allison not only believed that Jesus would show up, but she also put her faith into action.

Here's a great way to kickstart your journey:

- Begin with prayer

    If you have a desire or dream, the best way to get started is through prayer. Take it to Jesus every day, and don't be afraid to persist, even if it feels like He's not listening. Rest assured; He is. Approach Him boldly in prayer, day after day, until you receive a word from God. Express your gratitude for His involvement in your life and declare your unwavering belief in His ability to act on your behalf. Remember, we mentioned the importance of maintaining a prayer list during your quiet time? Well, this is the perfect item to include on that list. As an example, this book was a long-standing item on my prayer list. Every day, I prayed, "Jesus, I have faith that this book will be published. I trust you to provide the right people and connections." As you pray, be honest about the desires in your heart and allow Jesus to show you what is from Him or not.

• Acquire a Physical Reminder

Having a tangible reminder can be incredibly beneficial. For Allison, it was boxes when she was believing for divine assistance in moving into a new house. If it's a house for you, maybe you buy a random key. If you aspire to get married someday, consider purchasing a wedding ring, and it doesn't have to be expensive. Let that ring serve as a physical reminder to pray for your future partner daily. You can pray, "Jesus, help me become the partner you want me to be, as I desire to be a valuable gift." If you're seeking healing, you might write down a scripture that promotes healing and place it on your bathroom mirror. Having a physical reminder will help you stay focused as you pray, wait, and believe. Lastly, a powerful way to boost your faith is through music. It can be a source of inspiration and encouragement on your journey. Go back and listen to that song Believe For It as I mentioned earlier in this chapter and let it stir up your faith.

PART 3:

LIVING FOR

THE SAVIOR

SINFUL NATURE VS. SPIRITUAL NATURE

Allison and I share a deep love for enjoying a good movie together, and among our absolute favorites are Disney classics. One particular gem that holds a special place in Allison's heart is "The Lion King."

No matter how many times we indulge in this cinematic drama, it never seems to get old. "The Lion King" is a timeless Disney classic that we make sure to revisit at least once every couple of years.

What intrigues me most about "The Lion King" is how the story remains steadfast. Scar, consumed by his hatred for Simba and his father Mufasa, the king, consistently plays the role of the villain.

Each viewing of the film stirs a sense of anger within me as I witness Scar's relentless animosity toward the father and son. Scar's sole mission is to sabotage their relationship and obliterate all that is beautiful. He goes to great lengths to enlist the aid of the unhinged hyenas in his evil plan.

Imagine if Scar were to succeed in his malevolent scheme. In his ideal world, both Simba and Mufasa would meet a tragic end, the Lion King would cease to exist, and Scar would reign supreme over what was once a sacred and flourishing land.

Fortunately, this bleak outcome never comes to pass. Thankfully, evil does not triumph, and Simba matures into a formidable leader. He confronts Scar and, along with the hyenas, brings them the defeat they so rightfully deserve.

The tale of "The Lion King" serves as a powerful comparison for the perpetual internal struggle that resides within us all. It showcases the presence of both a protagonist and antagonist, a good side and a bad side, a path of righteousness and one of darkness, a realm of purity and one of evil.

At first glance, you might find this notion bewildering. Questions may arise, such as, "What do you mean I'm engaged in a battle?" or "Who is the adversary I must confront?" or even "What outcomes await me in this internal struggle?"

The two most crucial questions we need to address are:

- Firstly, who are the sides in this conflict?
- Secondly, what is the path to victory?
- Scripture provides us with clear answers to these questions, enabling us to discern the parties involved and understand the path to triumph. It's reassuring to know that we are not powerless in this battle; we possess significant inner strength.

THE TWO SIDES

Prior to our salvation, this conflict did not exist because we were ignorant of any other way. We simply indulged our own desires and pursued personal pleasures without hesitation. When we experience the saving grace of Jesus Christ by placing our faith in Him, a profound internal struggle begins.

The two opposing forces locked in battle within us are our flesh and our Spirit. These two aspects of our being are entirely contradictory. It's important to recognize that being saved through Jesus doesn't negate our humanity. We retain our human nature, desires, and inclinations.

We are still inherently self-centered beings who seek pleasure and gratification. This is an inherent aspect of our human nature, and we cannot deny or alter it; it's our "Scar." Our Scar is constantly scheming to satisfy our selfish desires, sometimes even at the expense of ourselves and others.

The other part of us is the Holy Spirit, a newer addition that came into existence when we accepted Jesus into our hearts. This is our "Mufasa," the good side, the divine power within us.

Making the faith-filled decision to accept Jesus awakened this new facet of our existence, and it's crucial that we understand it in the midst of this ongoing battle.

The Holy Spirit is God's power and presence dwelling within us after we accept Him as our Lord and Savior. The Holy Spirit is that inner awakening you experience when singing worship songs, the peace you feel during quiet times, and the gentle promptings guiding your actions. The Holy Spirit's primary purpose is to mold us into a likeness of Jesus. It continually urges us toward holiness, so we may mirror our Savior as closely as possible.

If you've been following Jesus, chances are you've sensed an internal struggle taking place within you. Perhaps you've become more conscious of your thoughts and actions or gained clarity in making wise choices. These experiences are not coincidental; they are manifestations of the ongoing battle. This war, as you can see, pits two fundamentally opposite sides against each other.

The flesh is inherently selfish, while
the Spirit is inherently selfless.

The flesh does not align with holiness or honor God. In stark contrast, the Spirit gently nudges us toward holiness and desires to honor God in all aspects of our lives.

MADE TO BE FREE

We weren't designed to live in captivity to our Scars. We are God's children, meant to embrace a life of joyful freedom. The flesh represents bondage, while the spirit signifies liberation. Choosing the flesh means living solely for our own desires, while embracing the spirit leads us toward a life of true freedom.

Experiencing freedom in Christ is infinitely more fulfilling than self-centered living.

When we live to satisfy our own desires, it only results in more and more bondage. Let's face it; we make rather inadequate gods of ourselves. Essentially, that's what we are to ourselves before we find salvation in Jesus—following our own desires as if we were gods.

The problem with this approach is its transience. It's unsatisfying because life is far from perfect, despite the façade of perfection often displayed on social media. Chasing after money will only leave us wanting more. Seeking popularity guarantees that we'll never feel popular enough. Striving for the perfect appearance is a quest that will never be fulfilled. You may briefly find it, but it won't last. Pleasing others is an endless endeavor with no finish line. I've been there myself, thinking that pleasing people would earn me their friendship. I would bend over backward to do whatever they wanted, hoping to win their friendship. But it was never enough. They weren't true friends, and they didn't genuinely care about me. The pursuit was endless.

The highs always fade, the pleasure of lust eventually wanes, and the enlightenment from entertainment is fleeting. The things of this world can only provide momentary satisfaction, and that's all they ever will offer. Nothing in this life can replace Jesus, the one true and satisfying God. The freedom He desires for us, His children, is one of genuine fulfillment. Jesus wants us to find joy in His presence rather than chasing fleeting satisfaction.

Truly, pursuing Jesus is more liberating than chasing after our own desires. The book of Galatians sheds light on this internal struggle:

> You, my brothers and sisters, were called to be free. But do not use your freedom to indulge the flesh; rather, serve one another humbly in love. (Galatians 5:13 NIV)

Freedom is the calling for all of humanity. Jesus wants us to live completely unshackled from any chains that might hinder us in life. When we strive to gratify ourselves and chase worldly pleasures, we are, in reality, harming ourselves more than anything else. It's only after finding salvation that we can truly grasp this reality. Living for the freedom Jesus offers means understanding that His blessings far surpass any worldly pleasures.

Psalm 16:11 in the ESV version beautifully reminds us: "You make known to me the path of life; in your presence, there is fullness of joy, and at your right hand are pleasures forevermore."

It might seem counterintuitive at first: how can abstaining from our desires lead to greater happiness?"

This journey is lifelong, an art and discipline that requires Jesus at its core. It's a daily pursuit, something we'll delve into further in the next chapter. The more you learn to abide in Jesus and let Him be your source of joy, the easier this process becomes.

The book of Galatians offers deeper insight into living for freedom:

"So I say, walk by the Spirit, and you will not gratify the desires of the flesh. For the flesh desires what is contrary to the Spirit, and the Spirit what is contrary to the flesh. They are in conflict with each other, so that you are not to do whatever you want. But if you are led by the Spirit, you are not under the law" (Galatians 5:16-18, NIV).

Imagine these chains that weigh us down: chains of insecurity, chains of lies we hear from others, chains of lies we tell ourselves, chains of guilt and shame, chains of unforgiveness, chains of lust and envy. Jesus desires to see you living a joy-filled, free life with no chains holding you down.

Freedom stands in opposition to indulging the flesh. Indulging the flesh means yielding to its desires, often far from what Jesus would want. For instance, the flesh might tempt you to live in slavery to it so it will make you want to gossip, saying, "It will feel good to talk badly about them; they were mean to you." It may encourage you to be insensitive in relationships, thinking, "It's OK to go out with as many people as you want, without regard for their feelings." Or it might tempt you to indulge in unhealthy eating, ignoring your health. Living in bondage to the flesh is impossible to recognize until we place our trust in Jesus and He reveals it to us.

FIGHTING FROM VICTORY

The daily practice we're discussing here revolves around understanding that we're not battling from a place of defeat but from a stance of victory. We're not trapped in a pit, struggling to climb out by doing the right things every day; that's not our situation.

Because we're saved and transformed through Christ, we've already conquered death! Eternal life is ours, and we'll never face death again! We are the victors, and the grand battle has already been won! We are not victims, my friend, we are victors!

However, our journey on earth requires us to persist through daily temptations. Shifting your mindset from defeat to victory is immensely powerful. If you perceive yourself as fighting for victory every day, it can feel like you're losing the battle repeatedly.

This is a guaranteed way to become disheartened. Jesus doesn't want us to live as if we're in chains; change your perspective to this: "I am a loved child of God with victory in Christ. Sin and temptation do not control me; in Jesus's name, I have authority over them."

When Jesus was crucified, He paid the price for our sins in full. We don't have to carry the weight of sin and its consequences each day. The enemy wants you to believe that victory is unattainable. Nothing is more dangerous to the enemy, and I mean absolutely nothing, than a child of God who comprehends their worth in Jesus and boldly walks in the freedom He provides.

Learning to resist our sinful desires and embracing the freedom Christ offers is a crucial aspect of being a new creation. It means leaving behind your old self and embracing your new life in Christ.

Nothing is more dangerous to the enemy than a child of God who knows their worth and walks boldly in freedom.

We all bear scars; there isn't a person who has lived or is currently living that doesn't grapple with inner scars. Everyone has at least one scar, if not multiple, that seeks to bring them down. Regardless of how put-together someone may appear on the outside, how flawless their social media presence is, or how close-knit their family may seem, they too have scars. These scars don't have to overcome us.

Remember, in the movie, who emerges victorious? Simba! The child of the king. We can attain this victory by living in the freedom that Jesus offers us.

In the upcoming chapters, and throughout the rest of this book, we will delve into what it means to live for Jesus. How does living for Jesus influence our daily decisions, actions, and habits? All of these aspects will be thoroughly explored.

Never forget, my friend, that you are already victorious, and the best is yet to come!

MOMENT OF REFLECTION

- Have you ever thought about what it truly means to live in the freedom that Jesus offers? Living in the freedom He provides isn't just a passive state of being; it's an active choice we make daily.

- In what ways can you identify your flesh in contradiction to Jesus?

- What does it mean to you to know you are fighting from victory and not for victory?

- Lastly, how can you remind yourself that you're not fighting for victory, but from victory? Sometimes, it's easy to forget that Jesus has already won the battle. To help yourself remember, immerse yourself in His Word, surround yourself with fellow believers, and spend time in prayer. These practices will strengthen your faith and keep you grounded in the truth that victory is already yours through Him.

DAILY BATTLES

When a nation anticipates the onset of a war, its preparations commence long before the first shot is fired. These preparations encompass diplomatic, economic, and, most crucially, military aspects. The military gears up in various ways, such as relocating aircraft to strategic positions, strategizing drone attacks, planning raids, or amassing troops in a massive buildup before an invasion.

Their readiness is geared toward enduring a protracted conflict, spanning many months, years, or even decades in extreme cases.

Douglas MacArthur, a highly esteemed and decorated American military general, once imparted this wisdom about going to war: "It is fatal to enter a war without the will to win it."

MacArthur underscores the necessity of unwavering determination for the fight. When a nation embarks on a war, it must be resolute in its commitment to triumph, no matter the cost. It must be prepared to make any sacrifice required.

THE BATTLE WE ARE FIGHTING

Though the war may already be won and we have victory and the outcome predetermined, a relentless battle unfolds here on earth. This is a struggle we shall engage in throughout our lifetimes.

Until our final breath, we confront a daily battle against succumbing to our own desires, as discussed in the preceding chapter. The battle of flesh vs spirit is real and it's a daily battle. Armed with the knowledge that we are fighting from victory, we have what it takes to not give in.

Triumphing in these daily battles necessitates a readiness to stand resolute and resist temptation's persistent pull toward sin. This may seem daunting, but we are not alone in this struggle. We have Jesus, whose Holy Spirit dwells within us, aiding us in resisting temptation. Additionally, we have the support of a community, a topic we will delve into in the upcoming chapter.

Returning to the verse in the Book of Galatians that illuminates this battle's nature:

For the flesh desires what is contrary to the Spirit, and the Spirit what is contrary to the flesh. They are in conflict with each other, so that you are not to do whatever you want. (Galatians 5:17 NIV)

This battle I refer to is the internal strife between your emotions, thoughts, and sinful desires. These are the temptations to sin, desires that the devil seeks to exploit, pushing you toward actions that will leave you feeling embarrassed and ashamed.

SIN DEFINED

Often, we have misconceptions about sin. Let me offer a clear definition to ensure we're on the same page: Sin is anything that obstructs our wholehearted worship of God.

In fact, the Bible straightforwardly states, "If anyone knows what they should do and doesn't do it, that is sin for that person." Sin is anything that hinders us from surrendering our entire heart to God, impeding our worship. The nature of these temptations may vary from person to person, but the fundamental concept remains the same.

Even as I write this, I feel conviction because I, like all, fall short daily. I am far from perfect. I will never be perfect. Perfection is an unattainable goal that we are not meant to achieve because Jesus has already achieved perfection for us.

We don't have to be perfect because
Jesus is perfect for us.

The more time we spend with Jesus, He transforms us inside and out to be like Him. We'll grow more like Him in our thoughts, actions, and words. We can, in fact, become increasingly more like Jesus and lead lives of purity that honor God.

A KING THAT CONFRONTED SIN

In the Bible, we encounter the story of King Josiah, a newcomer to the throne. He had recently assumed leadership in his kingdom and quickly identified a significant issue plaguing his land. His subjects harbored something in their lives that hindered their wholehearted devotion to God.

King Josiah's response to this challenge holds valuable lessons for us, offering guidance in our daily struggles to follow Jesus more closely.

Josiah, who ruled Jerusalem for an impressive thirty-one years, noticed a troubling problem among his people. They were engaging in the worship of an Asherah pole—a towering structure characterized by a birdlike figure perched at its pinnacle, adorned with wings.

It might have resembled something like this:

Figure 176.

Isn't it interesting how, at one point in history, people revered things other than God? A time when they placed their faith in material objects. It might not sound unfamiliar. Just like Josiah's people once worshiped an object other than God, we often face similar challenges in our lives. Josiah's reaction serves as a crucial example of how we can respond.

Our journey begins in the book of 2 Kings, where Josiah renews God's covenant with his people, emphasizing their commitment to love God above all else:

Standing by a pillar, the king solemnly renews this covenant in the presence of the Lord, pledging to follow His commands with all his heart and soul, reaffirming the words of the covenant written in a sacred book. The people, in turn, commit themselves to this covenant (2 Kings 23:3 NIV)

Josiah's determination to love God deeply is evident. He goes to great lengths to ensure he fulfills this command.

When he learns of his people's worship of the Asherah pole, his initial reaction is swift and resolute:

He removed the Asherah pole from the temple of the Lord, taking it to the Kidron Valley outside Jerusalem, where he burns it, grinds it to powder, and scatters the dust over the graves of common people. (2 Kings 23:6 NIV)

Josiah's immediate action is remarkable. He didn't convene a meeting, write a letter, or seek permission; he simply did what he knew was right. He understood the importance of removing distractions that led his people away from God and wasted no time in doing so.

What we see in Josiah is a demonstration of swift and consistent action. It takes immense courage to act as he did. He recognized that the current situation did not honor God and was detrimental to his people's hearts. Josiah boldly and courageously did what was necessary.

After Josiah's determined efforts to remove the Asherah pole from the temple, the Bible commends him, stating that:

There was no king before or after him who turned to the Lord with such dedication, heart, soul, and strength, in accordance with all the Law of Moses. (2 Kings 23:25 NIV)

This account holds significance for us today. Josiah was a king who sought to bring honor and glory to God. He achieved this by utilizing what he had and doing what he could—following the commandment for God's people to love Him with all their heart, soul, and strength (see Deuteronomy 6:4 NIV).

King Josiah's story inspires us to identify and remove obstacles hindering our wholehearted worship of God. He took action out of love for God and love for his people—a powerful example for us to follow.

LOOKING AT OUR LIVES

Just as Josiah took action against the Asherah pole, we can confront the distractions in our own lives. While we may not have a physical idol to destroy, we all contend with forces that seek to divert our focus from God. It's our responsibility to recognize these influences and combat them, just as we face daily temptations as followers of Jesus.

You might wonder why you didn't experience this tension before your conversion. Well, back then, you followed your feelings, not Jesus. Now, as a follower of Jesus, you see the struggle between His purity and holiness and the often-impure nature of your body.

These battles may appear similar to one another, but they can also differ significantly from person to person. Sometimes, we don't bring these struggles upon ourselves; they come to us unexpectedly. It's crucial to acknowledge that not all our challenges are of our own making.

For instance, someone may have wronged you or inflicted harm upon you, perhaps even as a child. As a result, you carry anger and unforgiveness. This fight was thrust upon you. Alternatively, someone may have maliciously framed you at work, leading to your dismissal. Now, you struggle to maintain your peace and grapple with thoughts of revenge.

Perhaps you were introduced to drugs or alcohol at a young age, unaware of the consequences. Now, you battle with dependence on substances. Or maybe your seemingly happy marriage suddenly crumbled when your spouse left and initiated divorce proceedings.

Notice how these battles were not of your making, yet they bring about real, intense emotions. If you find yourself in such a situation, it's OK to struggle. Jesus sees you, loves you, and cares about what you're going through. However, He doesn't want you to remain in this struggle; He desires to help you overcome it.

Most of the time, though, our battles are against the things we grapple with, not those that come unexpectedly into our lives. Anything we fail to remove from our lives hinders our ability to wholeheartedly worship God.

So, how do we identify these temptations? How can we recognize what's trying to divert our attention from God, and how do we prevent it from happening? It may seem like a daunting task, continually saying no to ourselves.

However, we are not powerless in this endeavor. We have the Holy Spirit, God's powerful presence within us, to assist us. We also have friends who can provide support, as we'll explore in the next chapter, and we can draw wisdom from King Josiah's story to guide us.

Overcoming our temptations demands an attitude similar to General MacArthur's approach to war: "the will to win it." We can indeed fight valiantly for the freedom we have in Jesus.

MY DAILY BATTLE

I won't ask you to reveal your daily struggles if I'm not willing to share mine. I want to be vulnerable with you.

Insecurity is a battle I face and it's by far my biggest one. I wish it would just vanish, but unfortunately, it doesn't. I fight against it vigorously, but often, it gains the upper hand. I have methods and phrases I say to myself to help calm the insecurity in me but it's still difficult some days.

You might wonder why this is a daily battle for me and you probably resonate with this as well. For me, it's about wanting to be perceived positively by my peers, to be seen as wise, fun, energetic, and someone others enjoy spending time with. I think about this almost every time I'm talking with someone.

I can't count how many times I've engaged in conversations and secretly worried, "I hope they still want to be my friend," or "I hope they thought I was cool." If I accidentally say or do something hurtful, it's tough for me to let it go until I believe the other person is OK and that the relationship is in good standing.

In work meetings, I often find myself thinking, "What does everyone in here think of me? Am I doing a good job?" I get caught up in these thoughts, but in reality, who cares?

If I'm being completely honest with you, friend, I almost didn't publish this book because I was afraid of how you'd perceive me. This took a lot of encouragement, prayer and nudges from Jesus. There were moments when writing this where I would close my laptop and say "I'm done because no one cares and no one will read this."

All of this stems from a lack of trust in Jesus and a greater focus on myself than on Christ. That's what it boils down to. This hinders me from fully following Jesus because when I'm wrapped up in my insecurity, I'm centered on myself and how others perceive me instead how Jesus sees me. It's sinful to constantly compare myself to others and fret about what people think. It's a struggle I face regularly. I do have great days where I don't allow this to creep in because I've better learned how to fight this daily battle. But it does creep up more often than I would like it to.

YOUR BATTLES

Temptations, we all grapple with them—those sneaky inclinations that tug at our moral compass. They come in many forms, from the urge to unleash a torrent of curses at the reckless driver who cuts you off in traffic, to the allure of indulging in gossip, deceit, flirtation, or lust.

Sometimes, it's as simple as seeking solace in alcohol, striving for a certain number of likes and followers online, or succumbing to an addiction that promises fleeting satisfaction.

While I can't possibly catalog every temptation in existence, I want to help guide you in pinpointing your own. Consider these probing questions as a compass to navigate the labyrinth of your desires:

- What actions am I often compelled to undertake, even though I question their propriety?

- Do these impulses run counter to the values of holiness and purity that define God's character?

- If my actions involve others, am I truly loving them in the best way possible?

- Will these choices lead to harm, either to me or those around me?

- Would I still follow through with my impulses if someone else were present to witness my actions?

- Am I comfortable sharing the details of my private life with my community, or would I be filled with embarrassment?

- Are my choices motivated by serving God, or are they merely serving my own desires?

By introspecting and honestly answering these questions, you can better understand and confront your temptations, ultimately steering your life toward a path of greater virtue and fulfillment.

I want to clarify upfront that I'm not here to make you feel bad or guilty; that's not my intention at all. My aim is to assist you in reaching a point where you can identify what might be hindering your progress in your relationship with Jesus. Sometimes, we have these invisible chains holding us back, and we don't even realize it until we stop and reflect.

If you're currently experiencing thoughts or a sense of heaviness in your heart, then you're on the right path. It's not about shame; it's likely Jesus revealing what's holding you back.

The nudges you feel right now or when you do something wrong are God trying to get your attention. That is one way God shows discipline toward us is by convicting us and correcting us of our sin. Conviction is vastly different from condemnation. Conviction is from God while condemnation is from the enemy. It's when you don't feel anything either right now or after you sin that I would start to wonder about your connection to God.

God's correction is a reminder of His connection.

King Josiah also used similar questions as a filter. He recognized that the actions of his people in his kingdom weren't honoring God and were causing harm, although they couldn't see it because they were pursuing their own desires. Hezekiah understood that to love his people and honor God, he needed to remove the sin that had entangled them.

Remember, our goal is simply to live in a way that honors and pleases God to the best of our abilities. No one is perfect, and perfection isn't the objective. If you make perfection your goal, you'll be disappointed because in God's kingdom, merit holds no value; grace is the only currency, and you have an abundance of it.

Our aim is to align our lives with Jesus and heed the nudges from the Holy Spirit. Every day, we face a choice: to say yes to the flesh (our own desires) or yes to the Spirit. You can only pursue one at a time; it's impossible to chase after sin and Jesus simultaneously.

Let me tell you, when you choose Jesus as your source of satisfaction, your joy will multiply tenfold. The key is shifting your desires from the flesh to an everlasting longing to love God, please Him, and find joy in the Spirit.

As Romans 8:5 (NIV) reminds us, "Those who live according to the flesh have their minds set on what the flesh desires, but those who live in accordance with the Spirit have their minds set on what the Spirit desires."

Let's dive into the practical steps you can take once you've pinpointed your temptations. There's a straightforward approach that can make a significant impact on your thoughts and actions.

Firstly, start by taking consistent action. When you repeatedly follow these two essential steps, you'll begin to witness a noticeable shift in your behavior.

What will transpire is a gradual reduction in the power your temptations hold over you. It's crucial to acknowledge that being tempted is a natural aspect of our human existence, and it may never completely disappear. However, by consistently practicing these two actions, you'll find that your desires and temptations gradually lose their grip on you.

DO WHAT YOU CAN DO

The first step in conquering our temptations, once we've identified them, is to take immediate action. This action should be tangible and something we can do right away. Here are a few examples:

If you're tempted to look at pornography, consider removing or limiting access to the device you use to watch it, whether it's a TV, phone, tablet, or something else. I once knew a friend who struggled with this and took the bold step of trading his iPhone for a basic flip phone that only allowed calls and texts.

He eliminated the temptation. Nowadays, there are even apps that can send a text message to someone you trust if they detect you searching for inappropriate content. If this one is yours, consider one of those actions that will help you.

If you find yourself tempted to curse people out when they anger you, the best course of action is to walk away from the situation. It may be difficult, but it's the right thing to do. If there's a particular person who consistently upsets you, consider distancing yourself from them or ending the friendship altogether. Removing the source of your anger can help eliminate the temptation. While we should love everyone, we don't have to maintain friendships that lead us into sin. If this involves a spouse, it's a different conversation, but for friends or acquaintances, it's a viable option.

Now, let's address insecurity. To combat feelings of insecurity, I often use the affirmations I shared in the "Talking to Jesus" chapter. Throughout the day, I remind myself, "I am a loved child of God, a loving husband, a leader who empowers, creative and innovative, and God's radiant love shines through me." These simple actions are tangible and make a significant difference in my life. I've set up reminders on my phone to reinforce these affirmations and remind myself of my worth and value in Jesus. I've shared this with people I trust as well. These small but consistent efforts can help you combat insecurity as well.

Lastly, one of the most practical ways to combat any temptation is by being part of a community. Having a group of godly people in your life can make all the difference. Being in a community provides encouragement from friends who genuinely care about you and accountability from people who want to help you navigate life. It gives you a group to celebrate your victories and support you during tough times. Community is essential for living a life connected to the heart of Jesus.

If I haven't explicitly mentioned your specific temptation in this chapter, know that you can apply the same principles. Take action to remove the temptation and share it with your community. We're all in this together.

Let's conclude this step with some powerful scriptures from 1 Peter:

Dear friends, remember, you are just visitors here. Since your real home is in heaven, I urge you to keep away from worldly desires that wage war against your very souls. (1 Peter 2:11 NLV)

Be alert and clear-minded. Your adversary, the devil, is like a roaring lion, seeking someone to devour. (1 Peter 5:8 NIV)

Part of winning this battle is staying vigilant and sober-minded, as the verse above suggests. We must realize that toying with temptation and sin is like playing with fire—it always brings harm. There's always a cost.

It's foolish to hold a burning ember in your hand and expect not to be burned. Why engage in sin and hope for a positive outcome? It's not possible. Sin leads to death every time. A mentor at the ministry school I attended often reminded us, "Your sin is dead on the ground when you believe in Jesus. Don't reach down, pick it up, and try to nurse it back to life."

PRAY FOR WHAT YOU CANNOT DO

Fighting temptations often seems like an insurmountable challenge, a struggle we cannot overcome, no matter how hard we try. However, there is a vital component to battling these temptations that we must embrace: prayer. Through prayer and invoking the name of Jesus, we access a wellspring of power beyond our own.

Prayer can serve as our lifeline in these moments of weakness. We can pray for the chains of addiction to shatter, beseech Jesus for His dominion over the areas where temptation thrives, and implore Him to be our strength.

It is within the comforting words of Jesus, whispered through our prayers, that we unearth the fortitude essential for triumphing over these battles. As we delve deeper into prayer, we discover that one of the fruits of the Spirit is self-control, a quality that grows within us as we draw nearer to Jesus.

As Galatians 5:22-23 (NIV) reminds us, "But the fruit of the Spirit is love, joy, peace, forbearance, kindness, goodness, faithfulness, gentleness, and self-control."

In the midst of your struggles, do not flee from God. He yearns to be your guiding light, a loving father, not a disappointed judge. His affection extends to your emotions, thoughts, circumstances, choices, and the course of your life. Take your burdens to Him in prayer, lay them at His feet, and let His comforting presence envelop you.

Whatever the battle is, know that the solution doesn't begin with someone sternly telling you to quit. It commences with you turning to your Heavenly Father. Confide in Him, beseech His aid in breaking these chains, and utter the prayers we've outlined above. Then, reach out to a trusted confidant and share your struggle.

MOMENT OF REFLECTION

Remember this: God is good, and His grace abounds for you. He is a loving father. He yearns to walk beside you through your trials. So, be resolute in your fight against the desires of the flesh; resist the temptation to live recklessly. Life holds more profound purpose than yielding to carnal whims. Jesus extends an offer of everlasting joy in His presence—a far superior reward.

- In closing, I want to share a passage from the book of Psalms that underscores the notion of battling and prevailing with God by your side:

He trains my hands for battle; my arms can bend a bow of bronze. You make your saving help my shield, and your right hand sustains me; your help has made me great. You provide a broad path for my feet, so that my ankles do not give way. I pursued my enemies and overtook them; I did not turn back till they were destroyed. I crushed them so that they could not rise; they fell beneath my feet. You armed me with strength for battle; you humbled my adversaries before me. You made my enemies turn their backs in flight, and I destroyed my foes. They cried for help, but there was no one to save them—to the Lord, but he did not answer. I beat them as fine as windblown dust; I trampled them like mud in the streets. You have delivered me from the attacks of the people; you have made me the head of nations. People I did not know now serve me, foreigners cower before me; as soon as they hear of me, they obey me. They all lose heart; they come trembling from their strongholds. (Psalm 18:34-45 NIV)

- Let us conclude with a heartfelt prayer:

Jesus, help me conquer these temptations and deepen my love for you. May your presence flourish within me, igniting a new fire, Holy Spirit, infuse me with a fresh love for God's Word and empower me to resist the temptations that assail me. Grant me the strength to remove these temptations from my life and to share my struggles with my community. My love and reliance rest upon you, Jesus. Amen.

DON'T FIGHT ALONE

In 2021, the Los Angeles Rams, an NFL football team was on the rise. The Rams were already showing promise, steadily improving day by day, but it was evident that they were missing a crucial element. It was as if they lacked that one final piece of the puzzle, a star quarterback.

The answer came in the form of Matthew Stafford, who had been playing for the struggling Detroit Lions. Stafford just couldn't seem to mesh well with the Lions and they never quite were in sync as a team with Stafford.

If you're familiar with the Lions, you know they've had their share of challenges—including their notorious Thanksgiving Day losses which stands at seven in a row at the time of this writing.

With Stafford's arrival to the Rams, everything began to shift. Stafford, who had been toiling away on a struggling team, found himself in an environment brimming with positive energy and immense potential. The Rams had finally found their missing piece, and their ascent to the top of the NFL was swift. In 2022, they clinched victory in the Super Bowl with Stafford as their quarterback.

It's truly captivating how one missing piece can have such a profound impact. This isn't just true in the NFL; it resonates with life as well. Missing one crucial element can make or break an NFL season, just as it can influence the course of our lives.

In 2015, while I was enrolled at NewSpring College, Jesus was transforming my life immensely. He was growing me in ways I didn't even know I could grow. However, during that transformative journey, something crucial was absent, preventing me from fully embracing life to the fullest. I was missing a vital piece of the puzzle to the full life Jesus wanted for me and you as well.

What I lacked was fundamental to my identity and my journey in life. Virtually everything revolves around this missing piece, and because it was absent, I found myself straying from the path that Jesus had called me to walk.

That missing piece was community, the presence of a group of people to do life with.

One key reason why community is so crucial is that who we hang out with shapes who we are becoming. You might have heard the saying, "Show me your friends, and I'll show you your future." Well, I've found that to be undeniably true. Surrounding ourselves with the right community is essential for experiencing life to the fullest during our time on earth.

In my personal journey, I believe that community was the final piece or "ingredient" I needed in my walk with Jesus. Not that community would make my life perfect but allow me to live a fuller life as Jesus intends us to live.

The absence of community allowed the enemy to creep into my life in subtle ways, undermining my actions and leading me toward anger, division, and self-centeredness instead of embracing Jesus's call to love others wholeheartedly.

FOUR FRIENDS IN A BATTLE

In the book of Exodus, we encounter a story of four friends locked in a fierce battle against a group known as the Amalekites. These friends were Moses, Joshua, Aaron, and Hur, who all belonged to the Israelite community.

As the Amalekites launched their attack, Moses turned to Joshua with a powerful directive. He said, "The Amalekites have descended upon the Israelites at Rephidim. Joshua, assemble a group of our men and confront the Amalekites in battle. Tomorrow, I will ascend to the hilltop with the staff of God in my hands" (Exodus 17:8-9 NIV).

Moses issued these orders and proceeded to the nearby hill, a remarkable act of faith. What's truly remarkable is his pledge to hold his staff aloft—a symbolic gesture signaling victory for the Israelites. Check out what happens next in this battle:

So Joshua fought the Amalekites as Moses had ordered, and Moses, Aaron and Hur went to the top of the hill. As long as Moses held up his hands, the Israelites were winning, but whenever he lowered his hands, the Amalekites were winning. (Exodus 17:10-11 NIV)

Joshua courageously engaged the Amalekites as Moses had commanded, while Moses, accompanied by Aaron and Hur, made his way to the hilltop. The outcome of the battle was closely tied to the position of Moses's uplifted hands.

Now, picture this: Moses, with his hands in the air, signifying victory when elevated and defeat when lowered. Yet, Moses, like any of us, felt the strain of holding something aloft for an extended period. Can you imagine how weary you'd become if you held a heavy object high in the air? It's only human. Observing this, Aaron and Hur, who were by Moses's side, recognized his fatigue and frustration. Here's what unfolded:

When Moses's strength waned, they took a stone and placed it beneath him, and he sat upon it. Aaron and Hur stood on either side, supporting his hands, ensuring they remained steadfast until the sun set. Thus, Joshua triumphed over the Amalekite army with his sword. (Exodus 17:12-13 NIV)

Aaron and Hur intervened, demonstrating remarkable solidarity with their weary leader. They didn't merely stand idly by, hoping Moses would persevere on his own. Instead, they took action, and they supported their friend in his time of strain.

This story teaches us a profound lesson: when individuals come together in the name of God to support one another, incredible things can unfold. Each of us, like Moses, will experience weariness, anger, frustration, and low spirits at some point in our lives.

In those moments, we all require an Aaron and a Hur—people who recognize our need and are willing to lend their strength when ours falters. Together, we can overcome the battles that life throws our way.

MY FRIEND NAMED SAM

During my time at NewSpring College, I had the privilege of meeting some truly remarkable individuals. It was a profound blessing to be surrounded by people of such integrity. These were individuals who genuinely cared about the person I was developing into and the future that Jesus was shaping me for.

The impact of the church leaders in my life was immeasurable, and I suspect that many of them may not fully grasp the extent of their influence in my life. To anyone reading this who was part of the church staff or shared this educational journey with me, I want to express my deepest gratitude. I recognize that I could never adequately repay the investment you made in me. I try to honor your investment by passing onto others the same investment you made in me.

Because of these people and their investment in me, I am who I am today. I wholeheartedly believe that I would not be where I am in life if not for the love of Jesus shining brightly through these leaders.

Among the incredible people I encountered during this period, there was one who stood out—Sam. Sam possessed a heart of tremendous compassion, and his concern for others was truly exceptional. It was during my second year in the program, as I continued to forge connections with more people, that I grew particularly close to Sam.

Sam was unlike any friend I had ever known before, and he played a pivotal role in my life. On a day when I was feeling down, Sam approached me with unfiltered honesty. He pointed out something crucial that I had been missing in my life: community. Community beyond leaders in the church. Community meaning a small group of people to gather with and share everything about life in a safe environment.

He explained that without a supportive community to encourage, uplift, and hold me accountable, I would never live life to the fullest. Sam's words were real to me. I understood what he was talking about. At the time I didn't have this kind of relationship in my life. It was exactly what I was missing.

Sam extended a generous invitation for me to join the community he was a part of—an assembly of about twenty guys our age who met regularly to care for one another. Initially, I was hesitant and uncertain about what to expect.

At the time, Sam's group was already established, but I decided to accept his invitation. Looking back, I am profoundly grateful that I did. My first experience with the group, which we referred to as "home group" at the time, was nothing short of eye-opening.

It became immediately evident that I had found what had been missing in my life, and I knew I was exactly where I needed to be. For this realization, I owe Sam an immense debt of gratitude.

A friend like Sam is a rare and invaluable treasure, a reminder that we all need someone like him in our lives.

On my first night at the home group, I found myself in a room filled with around fifteen or twenty guys, all aged between eighteen and twenty-five. We engaged in a nearly two-hour conversation about the happenings in our lives. We took turns sharing what weighed on our hearts and sought prayers for those concerns. I was genuinely astonished.

These guys were opening up and sharing things I wouldn't have had the courage to discuss with anyone else. I distinctly remember one guy admitting, "I've stopped making unwise choices because I don't want to show up at the group next week and have to explain my actions to everyone." That, right there, is what we all need—accountability. They were showing me that vulnerability was a sign of strength.

I used to think that keeping everything bottled up inside was the way to navigate life, but this moment was proving me wrong. When we move through life unchecked, without anyone questioning our choices, we often end up making decisions we never thought we would.

I once heard a pastor say, "Sin will always take you farther than you want to go, make you stay longer than you want to stay, and make you pay more than you want to pay." He was absolutely right. Without a supportive community, that's precisely what happens to us. I thank God for people like Sam.

Vulnerability is a sign of strength, not weakness.

Although I was welcomed by guys I didn't even know that night I felt welcomed into a family. Sam had taken me to a place where I could be genuine and honest about myself, and it was truly beautiful. That was the only place where I could find belonging—the missing ingredient I had been searching for.

We were not created to be alone, no matter how introverted we might be, including me. We were designed to be in community with one another and with God. I've discovered that the more I tried to tackle life on my own, the more complicated it became.

I think a common misconception is that if we elect to become a part of a group it means something is "wrong" about us.

What I found to be true is that these guys weren't there because something was "wrong" in their lives; they were there because they understood that they weren't meant to navigate life alone. They got it, and I desperately needed it. They had become better men because of their community, understanding the significance of this verse found in Scripture:

Bear one another's burdens, and so fulfill the law of Christ. (Galatians 6:2 NIV)

We are called to walk alongside each other and care for one another. Life is tough, and Jesus knew that, which is why we have the privilege of gathering with people who will be there for us.

Our culture may not always applaud this kind of living. Admitting that you are part of a group that holds you accountable may not be the coolest thing in the world because the world tells us that we are strong enough to handle life on our own. It tells us that we don't need the help of others. It tells us that it doesn't matter if we sin. All of which could not be further from the truth.

Consider this scenario: What if you were part of a group of people who didn't judge you, no matter what you shared with them? Instead, they genuinely cared about you and were always willing to lend a helping hand when you needed it?

Imagine having a support system in your life that stood by your side during moments of tragedy, offering comfort and companionship.

What if there was a circle of individuals who loved you deeply and were ready to assist you whenever you needed it?

I never realized the absence of community in my life until I had it, which is quite peculiar when you think about it.

By embracing my purpose and living as a new creation within a community, I discovered a newfound sense of freedom in my life.

Within our community, authenticity and honesty reign supreme. It's a safe haven where we can be our true selves, without the need for pretense. Here, we are met with both grace and truth, surrounded by people who genuinely care about our well-being.

Community is essential if we want to live life to the fullest.

While I may no longer be enrolled in ministry college, I continue to experience authentic community in my life. Just as I had Sam when I was in college, I have maintained connections with individuals who offer support and accountability. I've also made efforts to join other groups, recognizing the transformative power of having a community that holds you accountable, prays for you, and offers encouragement.

MY FRIEND GROUP

I'm part of a close-knit group consisting of around seven individuals, and we make an effort to spend quality time together whenever possible. This group has brought immense joy and value to my life, much like how Sam was a vital part of my previous season during ministry school.

I cherish my friendship with this group immensely. They provide me with encouragement, love, support and lots of laughs. Our gatherings often involve shared meals, card games at someone's house and heart-to-heart conversations about the happenings in each other's lives.

Our friend group rallies around one another during difficult times, celebrates each other's victories, and provides steadfast support throughout life's ups and downs. We've been there for each other during joyful celebrations and tearful moments. It's remarkable how this community radiates beauty, and one of the things I cherish the most is the absence of judgment among us.

SMALL GROUP:

Allison and I are part of a small group at our church as well. When we come together with our group, we engage in heartfelt conversations about our lives, how we can support and serve one another, and offer prayers to help shoulder each other's burdens. Essentially, we're there for each other, no matter what.

Our discussions often revolve around scripture and how we can live out our faith. We also dive into the messages delivered at church and brainstorm ways to apply them in our daily lives.

If I rewind to my days in ministry college, I never imagined I'd find such a sense of community and be able to be truly open and vulnerable. Now, I'm fortunate to be a part of not just one, but two incredible community groups—my circle of friends and the group I'm connected with through our church.

It all began when Sam invited me to join his group painting the picture of what I was missing, helping me understand what real community is supposed to look like. I now have Aarons and Hurs in my life and I couldn't be more grateful for them.

MOMENT OF REFLECTION:

- Who are your Aaron and Hur's? Do you have a group of friends like this in your life? A place where you can be your authentic self?

- If you haven't been invited into a group, let me offer some guidance on how to identify one. Take a close look at the people around you. Do you see anyone actively pursuing a relationship with Jesus and who can help keep you accountable? There may be people in your proximity that need community as well.

- Alternatively, if you share common interests like rock climbing, reading, biking, or tennis, seek out those who embody these qualities and connect with them. Common interests are great ways to get a group started.

- Remember, it doesn't have to be elaborate—simply gather for quality time focused on encouragement, prayer, and accountability. Keep in mind the purpose of community: we gather to become who Jesus wants us to be.

- If you can't find friends who possess these qualities, it might be time to reevaluate your current friendships. For some of us, gaining a genuine, godly community might mean saying no to certain relationships. Are there people in your life whom influence you in negative ways that you need to have an honest conversation with?

- Or, for you, the better question may be, can you be an "Aaron and Hur" to? Who do you know that needs you right now? Who has God placed in your life that could really use your care? Reach out to that person today, you'll be grateful you did.

- Let's close with a prayer:

  Jesus, help me to see how powerful community can be. Help me to find community and live life to the fullest this way. Help me to become more like you. Help me grow in honestly, vulnerability and integrity. Help me see the people in my life that I can be in community with. Help me see someone in my life that you want me to care for. In Jesus name, Amen.

LIVING ON A MISSION

Congratulations on reaching the final chapter of this book! I'm sincerely grateful to have you join me on this journey. My hope and prayer is that this book has truly enriched your walk with Jesus.

There's one more crucial aspect of living life to the fullest that I don't want to overlook—it's about living on a mission.

Have you ever been given a challenge or a special task by someone? Something of utter importance that maybe had consequences if you didn't do it? Maybe it was chores around the house while growing up. Taking out the trash, doing the dishes, and cleaning your room. All important things or the house will be a mess. Or maybe it's a task at work where there are deadlines to meet and customers to serve. Not completing the due dates will create backlogs and headaches for your team so, therefore, you feel the urgency and pressure to perform.

For me, I have a day that I was given a task. A responsibility to perform a duty.

I'll never forget the day I was commissioned at the church I work at. It was at an all-staff meeting, and I was asked to take on a significant charge. This charge was multifaceted—to share the Gospel, live a life that reflects Jesus, and wholeheartedly love God, His people, and support His church.

As this moment unfolded, I felt a deep sense of responsibility within my heart. I believed that I had a role to play in this mission, and I felt empowered to carry it out. The weight of this mission was real, as I felt my heart ache. With this mission came a duty to carry out but also a feeling of honor that I was getting to be a part of God's story.

OUR MISSION

Just as I felt a sense of ownership in that auditorium during my commissioning, Jesus commissions us when we accept Him as Savior of our lives. He entrusts us with a mission to fulfill during our time on this earth.

We're not just saved to lead godly lives until we pass away; we're not just saved as a get-out-of-hell ticket. He's given us a purpose—a mission that is of utmost importance. Something to truly embrace and take ownership of. A mission that demands we not be spectators in the stands, but we get out on the field.

This mission is for everyone, not just a select few. Not just for church staff or elders within a church. Not just for seasoned Christians, elderly Christians or younger Christians. But for everyone. Anyone who calls on the name of Jesus has a responsibility charged to them by Jesus to carry out this mission.

So, what did Jesus commission us with? What is it that He wants us to do? Jesus eloquently outlines His expectations for His followers, explaining what He desires for us to accomplish during our time here on earth.

Jesus was pressed to share what is the most important commandment that we are to follow. What was the one thing that rose above all other things for followers of Jesus? This question needed to be answered and Jesus knew it. So he shared what was most important to His heart.

First, Jesus said above all else, do this:

1.   Love God and love others

"The most important command," responded Jesus, "can be summed up in these words: 'Listen, O Israel: The Lord our God, the Lord is one. Love the Lord your God with all your heart, soul, mind, and strength.' The second commandment is equally important: 'Love your neighbor as yourself.' There is no greater commandment than these" (Mark 12:29-31 NIV).

Loving God wholeheartedly and then extending that love to others is the core of Jesus's teaching. His directive is not self-centered; it revolves around the idea of others.

However, it's crucial to understand that Jesus emphasized the priority of loving God first. He recognized that without a relationship with God that fills our hearts with love, peace, and joy, it becomes exceedingly difficult to love others as He desires. Without a love for Jesus, we don't have love to share with others. We cannot give love and grace that we do not have ourselves. This is why your quiet time with Jesus as we talked about earlier in this book is essential to your faith journey.

We cannot pour out into others what we do not have ourselves.

I urge you to have a daily time with Jesus every day. Listen to worship music often and do what it takes to have a heart of humility that's focused on Jesus. This is good soil for Jesus to do incredible works in your life.

It's remarkable that Jesus places great emphasis on loving the people around us. If we wholeheartedly love God and cultivate a strong relationship with Him through our daily quiet times, but at the same time, exhibit rudeness and meanness toward others on a regular basis, we miss a crucial element of following Jesus.

If Jesus lives in my heart, I must love others with all my heart.

This leads me to a question: is your life marked by love? Would others consider you to be someone that exudes love? People that interact with us will know if Jesus is in our hearts or not based on how well we love them.

Just as Jesus extends grace, we too must show grace. As He demonstrates compassion, we should exhibit compassion. His forgiveness should inspire our forgiveness toward others, and His provision should motivate us to fearlessly help those in need.

To gauge our alignment with Jesus's teachings, we can ask ourselves a simple question: "Am I loving this person the way Jesus instructs me to?"

2.   Spread the Gospel

In Matthew 28:19-20, Jesus imparts to us what is often referred to as "the great commission." It's not a mere suggestion but a vital commandment for us, His devoted followers. Similar to the commandment to love God and others, this one is nonnegotiable.

As followers of Jesus, we carry the profound responsibility of spreading the word about what Jesus has done in our lives. We are the bearers of the precious Gospel message, and if we don't share it, who will?

For me, that question is what created a sense of ownership in my heart. If I am not investing in the lives of others for the sake of the Gospel, who else will?

We have a duty to share the love of Jesus with others. This mission is personal to us, as we've experienced firsthand what Jesus has done in our lives. Why would we not share that with someone else?

One of the core motivators for not sharing the precious gift of salvation with others is fear.

Friends, fear has become our friend. We've cozied up to fear and let it control our emotions and actions.

Jesus has entrusted us with the task of sharing His message of hope and salvation with the people in our lives. The remarkable act of redemption He's performed in our lives, rescuing us from our sins and bestowing upon us hope and a promising future, isn't meant to remain hidden.

It's a gift meant to be shared with others, beginning with those already present in our lives. Consider this: Who has God brought into your life that you know hasn't yet encountered Jesus?

Let's take a moment to revisit Emma, the woman with a broken heart whom Jesus met at the well. She was living a life filled with shame and pain, yet Jesus approached her right where she was.

Jesus didn't shame or condemn her. Instead, He lavished her with love and grace. In the previous discussion about Emma's story, I omitted a significant part because I wanted to conclude this book with what transpired after her conversation with Jesus.

Here's what unfolded with Emma:

> After their conversation, Emma left her water pot and returned to the village, exclaiming to the people, "Come see a man who knew all about the things I did, who knows me inside and out. Do you think this could be the Messiah?" Intrigued, the villagers went to see for themselves. (John 4:28b-30 MSG)

It didn't stop with Emma sharing what had happened with others. The story continues unfolding with this:

> Many of the Samaritans from that village committed themselves to him because of the woman's witness: "He knew all about the things I did. He knows me inside and out!" They asked him to stay on, so Jesus stayed two days. A lot more people entrusted their lives to him when they heard what he had to say. They said to the woman, "We're no longer taking this on your say-so. We've heard it for ourselves and know it for sure. He's the Savior of the world!" (John 4:39-42 MSG)

The impact of Emma's testimony was profound. Many Samaritans from her village believed in Jesus because of her witness. They marveled at her words: "He knew all about the things I did. He knows me inside and out!"

Emma's response was remarkable. She shared with the entire town what Jesus had done for her. She didn't keep it to herself, nor did she restrict her story to a select few. If Emma had access to Facebook or Instagram, she might have gone live to share with everyone the extraordinary transformation Jesus had brought into her life.

Her heart overflowed with such joy that she couldn't contain it; she had to share it with everyone she encountered. The love that was beaming out from her could not be contained. It had to be shared and Emma knew it.

Loving others means sharing the message of Jesus.

Whether it's with your coworkers, family members, or anyone you know who doesn't have a relationship with Jesus, remember that the Gospel is meant for everyone, everywhere, and at all stages of life. No one ever outgrows it or graduates it.

You don't need to be a preacher, ordained, have attended seminary, or hold a certificate for this. In fact, all of that is unnecessary. Jesus never mentioned such requirements. Just share what Jesus has done for you, just as Emma did. Jesus has given each of us a story to share. It's a great story. The reason it's great is not because it's perfect, it's because it's our story. That's what makes it special. We are called to share what Jesus has done with us with our kids as we are the ones Jesus has entrusted that responsibility to. We are called to share what Jesus has done with our coworkers, with friends, with family, with people we see every single day who may be hurting on the inside desperate for hope. Jesus is hope! Jesus is too good to keep on the inside!

There is someone Jesus is wanting you to share your story with. I read a quote in a book in the summer of 2022 that hit me in the heart about writing this book that read, "Someone is waiting on you. Someone is waiting to read your life story."

Someone is waiting to hear your story.
Will you share it with them?

Go out there, love God, love people, and share the message of salvation.

Jesus said, "You are the light of the world. A city that is set on a hill cannot be hidden. Nor do they light a lamp and put it under a basket, but on a lampstand, and it gives light to all who are in the house. In the same way, let your light shine before others, so they can see your good deeds and glorify your Father in heaven" (Matthew 5:14-16, NIV).

MOMENT OF REFLECTION:

- Have you started having a daily time with Jesus? What does it look like for you?

- Would others know that you follow Jesus based on your actions toward them? What might need to change for you to be marked by love?

- You have a story to share. Your story is what Jesus has done in your life. Will you share that the people Jesus has placed in your life? Let this question sit with you for a moment as you think about the names of others you know. I encourage you to write these names down and let them be who you seek to share your story with.

- Closing prayer:

Jesus, help me to love you first and love others as you have loved me. Help me to follow you daily submitting my heart and yielding to your direction. Help me to have courage to share my story with the people you've placed in my life. Help me see that you are with me as I take this step. I pray for strength and guidance as I step out in bravery to share your love. In Jesus name, Amen.

ENCOURAGEMENT

Thank you again, friend, for going on this journey with me. There was a lot to cover throughout these pages and I hope you found the content helpful, insightful, uplifting, and enriching. My hope from the beginning was to encourage you, uplift you and lead you straight to Jesus, where life to the fullest begins.

I want you to know that your faith journey, if starting when you picked up this book, will indeed be a journey. It won't be all smooth skies and tailwinds as we pilots like to say.

A journey is filled with excitement, thrill, and smiles. These moments will happen tenfold for you as you follow Jesus. He desires great things for you, immeasurably more than all you can imagine!

This journey will also be filled with tears, heartache, and hardship as any journey worth trekking should be. Following Jesus doesn't guarantee an absence of or free pass from hardship. Tough times will come and that's OK. Tough times came before, but you were dealing with them on your own strength. Now when trials come that make your heart sink and make you want to crawl in bed and hide, you have the strength of Jesus with you. You won't be alone when you face difficulties any longer. Following Jesus with your life doesn't mean no difficult things but it does guarantee you'll have:

- A friend in the fire.

- A hand to hold when there's no one else to hold you.

- A guide who will give you wisdom that's priceless.

- A lion who will give you courage to face the trials of life.

Jesus will be those and so much more for you. He will always be by your side, even if in a moment it feels as if He may not be. He's there and always will be. He will hear your prayers and guide you through the rest of your life. Focus on having your daily quiet times and drawing near to Jesus. That time you are intentional in praying and listening to Him is invaluable. Run to that well every day and be filled with love, grace, truth, and guidance.

Turn to Him for everything on your journey. He is provider, sustainer, life-giver, forgiver, defender, protector, and He's always enough, always. He's never failing, and He promises to always be with you! Jesus is the one person that will never give up on you no matter what happens.

Jesus loves you, He cares for you, and I know that as you follow Him, your best days are ahead of you! Believe this with all of your heart along with me: The best is yet to come!

Cheering you on and praying for you in your journey,

Bryant

NEXT STEPS

You may be wondering "what do I do from here?" I want to help shed some light on that question for you here because following Jesus isn't meant to be confusing.

First, if you would like more content on following Jesus, visit my website where I write regularly about things I'm learning in my own faith journey. I've written about my own tough trials in life, I've written about spiritual practices I've learned, and I believe the content will further guide you in your faith journey. My thoughts are curated in helpful articles and devotionals that will be an additional resource to you. Visit:

www.bryantwestbrook.com

Baptism

If you are a new believer, I encourage you to get baptized by immersion. Expressing your faith in an outward way is one of the initial steps Jesus challenges us to take. Jesus went public in baptism and so should we. I believe it's important to do this after you have accepted Jesus into your heart, and you understand what salvation means to you.

Community

I encourage you to get a small group of people around you who will love you, encourage you, and challenge you. It is special to have a group of people to do life with. Like I said earlier in the book, I didn't know what all I was missing out on until I had it. Community is such a gift, and we need to embrace it and not run from it.

Service

I believe that Jesus has called us to a life of service as His followers. There is enriching joy waiting for you on the other side of service. There are many ways to serve others. This can be done on your own via serving the homeless in your community, visiting elderly in the community or giving financially toward a need someone has. While serving individually is a great and noble thing to do, I believe that serving through the local church is the best. There is something about being on a team of people all serving others for the glory of God! The beauty of the local church is that there are many ways to get involved. Picking up a shovel and putting it in the ground via your local church is so rewarding. Jesus wants to build His church through us. We are the church. The church isn't a building, it's us. What an honor to get to partake in this.

We are on this journey together, friend. I'd love for you to consider these next steps and apply them to your life just as I have my own.

ABOUT THE AUTHOR

Bryant's roots trace back to Lavonia, a cozy little town nestled in the northeastern part of Georgia. In his life, he holds a handful of passions: his faith in Jesus, his marriage to Allison, their beloved dog Riley, the big "C" church, the thrill of soaring through the skies as a pilot, and, of course, the spirited world of Clemson Tigers football.

CONNECT

Facebook: facebook.com/bryant.westbrook.5

Instagram: bryant_westbrook

Website: www.bryantwestbrook.com

9 798822 932913